ESSAYS ON CREATING SACRED RELATIONSHIPS

•

The Next Step in a New Paradigm

•

by Sondra Ray

CELESTIAL ARTS
Berkeley, California

Celestial Arts Publishing
P.O. Box 7123
Berkeley, California 94707

Cover and text design: Victor Ichioka
Front cover photo: Bruce Hortz
Printed in the United States

Library of Congress Cataloging-in-Publication

Ray, Sondra
    Essays on creating sacred relationships : the next step in a new paradigm / by Sondra Ray.
        p.   cm.
    Includes bibliographical references.
    ISBN 0-89087-796-3
    !. Marriage—Religious aspects. 2. Unmarried couples—Religious aspects. 3. Courtship—Religious aspects. 4. Spiritual life. I. Title
BL462.R38 1996
299'.93—dc20   96-6393
                                                                CIP

First Printing, 1996

I   2   3   4 / 99 98 97 96

DEDICATION

With great honor, I dedicate this book to my guru Shastriji, who is the High Priest of Babaji, MahaAvatar (our mutual Supreme Sadguru, total manifestation of God in human form, who is bringing spiritual rebirth to the planet).

Over many lifetimes, Shastriji, has taken me through darkness into light by assisting me in a step-by-step process to give up my personal, limited consciousness. He has showered upon me his spiritual energy and grace, which has empowered me to achieve that which seemed far beyond my normal consciousness.

Because I have had the great privilege and good fortune to be connected to this God-realized Master, Shastriji, and enter into his family like a daughter, the least I could do is to give back to society and humanity at large as much as possible, in any way possible, for the supreme grace I have been given.

With this spirit in mind, I acknowledge Shastriji, one of the purest beings on this planet. May everything I write be something beautiful for God.

A special thanks also to Meher Baba whose *Discourses* have given me so much spiritual understanding and inspiration for this.

I want to honor my recent and new female colleagues, Beth Hin and Leslie Temple Thurston who helped me create the space for what was to be done. I also want to honor my female guide in Spain, Elena Duranona, who helped me get going further and also Rich, the man I was with at the time, who cured me of writer's block among other things.

And special thanks to the women who took care of me while writing this: Jane, Liz, and Kerry, who provided me with a very sweet and holy setting in the Gold Coast, Australia; and who supported me emotionally and physically the whole time I worked on this book.

Bhole Baba Ki Jai!

ACKNOWLEDGMENTS

Robert Roskind, Robert Coon, The Hazelton Clinic, Robert Skutch and the Foundation for Inner Peace, Mary Daly, Scott Peck, Frank Pitman, Dion Fortune, Gary Zukav, Eleanora Coppola, Meher Baba, Yogananda, Ram Dass, Leonard Orr, Babaji, Diana Laschelles, Rajneesh, John Price, Judith Sills, Susan Faludi, Barbara de Angeles, Germaine Greer, Shastriji, Bob Mandel, *New Woman, Elle,* and *Ita.*

CONTENTS

PART II: ESSAYS ON ENLIGHTENED BUSINESS AND POLITICS

CLOSING

INTRODUCTION:
A NEW STATE OF MIND

"PURITY IS THE ONLY ACCEPTABLE STATE OF MIND."
I received these words from a Mayan goddess. I had just
been in Cancun, Mexico, with our Loving Relationship
Training group, now called the New Relationship Training.
While near the ruins of Tulum, where high priests were
trained, I had experienced the past lives of other Mayans,
so it was no wonder a goddess was lurking near me.

The goddess continued: "From purity comes honesty
. . . which leads to integrity . . . which leads to right
action." Though not really a new state of mind, it *feels*
new—especially after having "fallen" from a state of
grace and having entrenched ourselves in lifetimes of ego.
It is like being stricken with a horrible illness for years
and years and suddenly, with the help of a miracle, getting
well. It feels like another chance at life. Or it is like leaving
an abusive marriage and beginning a new one. It is still a
marriage, but one hopes that one can keep it pure and not
recreate the past. The message from the goddess crystal-
lized an idea and I continue to honor the wisdom of the
Mayans to this day.

We have all had moments where we have experienced
feelings of purity and holiness. But why could we not
maintain it? How do we recreate that state of mind? This
book is about a new model, or paradigm for relationships— the next step for male-female relationships.

The preparation for this project was long and difficult. I was overdue to write a book and totally frustrated
because I did not know what I was supposed to write. I

CREATING
SACRED
RELATIONSHIPS

had writer's block. I overcompensated to friends instead. I wrote and sent a continuous stream of faxes. This not only got very expensive, but it was also very hard on my various hosts—and over-taxed their fax machines. My energy was chaotic, wild—I could not sleep. I would pace until 3 or 4 a.m. and write long faxes on this or that. I am talking about really long faxes. My friends would get up in the morning to find reams of paper cascading out of their machines and across the floor.

I went to Spain to rest and to live with my LRT producer, Adolfo. I set aside three weeks just to write. When finally Adolfo's fax broke down, he asked our guide, Elena, to come over and do prayers and cleanse the flat. Things were really chaotic the morning before she came: the telephones, my computer, the fax machine, all of our electrical equipment was down.

When Elena arrived, we laid all our problems at her feet. She was so calm, so loving. She sat there, after making the long climb up four flights of stairs , and smiled at us. She took in everything we said, and then she walked around the huge flat praying and sometimes singing. She put white flowers and candles in the corners. She threw flowers on us while we continued our work. Everything began to calm down. I knew the Divine was taking over; and something was going to happen. In the kitchen, Elena lit a Cuban cigar, smoked it, and spread the ashes around —her way of giving us the sacred ash. After she finished all this, we were told to leave everything as she had it for twenty-four hours.

She then came and sat in the office and looked at me. I said, "Do you have to leave?" She said, "No, I must stay longer." I could not believe it. I told her I wanted to start a book in her presence. If I could get the first page written, the rest would be no problem.

I thank Elena Duranona, who has been my spiritual

guide in Spain for several years. She always understood when to be tough on me and when to be very soft with me. There were times when she had to be very tough indeed; but I needed it.

In the past, I have been more comfortable with male teachers, I was so involved with my masculine side. I was out there "in the trenches," after all, integrating the New Age into the patriarchal systems of society. I was never part of the so-called feminist movement as such. But, in my own way, I have been a catalyst for change all along.

A friend encouraged me to meet a new spiritual guide named Beth Hin. On the day that I went to sit before Beth, she wasted no time with idle chatter. She began by saying, "They want you to create something beyond the Feminist Movement." "They" referred to the spiritual hierarchy. I was clueless about the rest. So I asked, "Could I please have more information?"

"No," she replied. "There is no more information. It has never been done. You have to channel it." Then she proceeded to tell me that I should do a ceremony on the following day and decide if I wanted to accept this mission. She emphasized during this session that I was embarking upon my "true destiny."

I set up an altar on the fireplace, sat before it, and wrote a prayer to the spiritual heirarchy. I told them I was willing to do this mission if, in fact, it was my true destiny. "Could you please give me more information?" I asked again. A sudden wind blew like a cyclone, throwing open the doors and windows. Startled, I asked the neighbors if they had seen or felt it. They did not know what I was talking about.

After this event, I experienced some paralysis in my left hip for almost two months. I guess I was terrified because I had committed to something I did not understand. Later, when I arrived at Babaji's ashram in India, I performed a ceremony with some close women friends by the Ganges. We bathed each other in oils and flowers and immersed ourselves in the river. I asked them to pray with me. We left the river and approached the Divine Mother Temple. (The "Dhuni" was built by my guru, Babaji himself, with his own hands.) I distinctly heard, *"Divine Mother Movement..."* Though startled again, I realized that the reason this creation was beyond the feminist movement was because it *included men.* Suddenly, my mission made some sense to me.

I travelled to an ashram in the Himalayas where I took part in a *navaratri* (nine days of continuous worship to the Divine Mother). I climbed to the five-thousand-year-old Divine Mother Temple in the mountains. My *puja* to the Divine Mother felt more direct this time, perhaps because here I was closer to Her.

At the end of the navaratri, my guru Shastriji put a tourniquet on my left arm for five minutes and shouted a mantra into my third eye. I had no idea what he was doing. Do you know how long five minutes is with a tourniquet on your left arm? I thanked him and bowed.

Then began a two-year process which was the hardest of my life. What I learned was this: People have strange reactions to change. Some revert to earlier modes of behavior, some get angry, and some leave. A person's true colors are revealed. It is not always pleasant. I started questioning my role as a catalyst for change and as a pioneer. I did not like this role at times—not at all. *But I stuck it out!* The rewards have been mind-blowing. I often wanted to quit because I felt totally alone as a pioneer. However, things happened that forced me to see that I was on the right path and there was no turning back.

In the spring of 1994, my astrologers told me that a particular planetary alignment was occuring that would begin the breakup of the Patriarchy, and start Divine Mother Energy flowing in to replace it.

That night, there was a miracle. My picture of the Divine Mother began emitting sacred ash. Two associates and myself witnessed this miracle and I invited them to join me in eating the ash. It was very sweet—like powdered perfume. It was then I knew for sure that I was on the right track. I often go back to that moment, that blessing, and remember the gift I was given.

Then I was presented with one of the biggest disappointments of my life. My organization seriously began to break up. I had become aware of my co-dependent and dysfunctional behavior that gave away my power. My awareness threw off the old "balance." Some people on my staff no longer supported what I was doing. I was devastated. I had to go forward alone.

In Santa Fe, I led the first Divine Mother Conference with the support of Beth Hin and Leslie Temple Thurston. This was the *real* initiation of the Divine Mother Movement. We had 130 women from North America and Europe.

What the Divine Mother has done for me is to give me a whole new life. The Divine Mother Movement is still like a baby. It is still unfolding. But the Divine Mother herself is pure *kundalini*. To surrender to her energy is truly awesome. My tests have been very big. Frequently, I have had to sit myself down and give myself a lecture that went something like this:

"Now, were you not one of the first Peace Corps volunteers? Even though it was hard, was it not one of the most rewarding experiences of your life? And were you not one of the first Rebirthers? Even though it was hard, did you not get all the benefits of that privilege? Are you quitting *now*?"

My desire to quit would then be over in about five minutes. I would get up and go on.

As one accumulates power, the ego can balloon up unless the personality is continuously and simultaneously incinerated. My old personality had to be "cleaned out." As the kundalini moved up through my *chakras*, I tried to resist it. There is an image of the Divine Mother with many arms that represents her taking your karmas. There is another image of her with a necklace of freshly severed human heads around her neck. The heads represent lust, anger, greed, envy, delusion, and fear. I have concluded that the Divine Mother chopped off my head to cure me.

Was I going to let the Divine Mother heal me and let her kundalini clean me out or was I going to keep it all suppressed? I knew if I chose suppression, it would just cause aging and death. I wanted to try for immortality. In India, they say, "She alone grants the boon of Physical Immortality." I understood that all the great immortal yogis prayed to the Divine Mother because there was no escape from the wheel of karma except by Her grace. I told Her I was willing to be born again. I craved the destruction of my limitations.

Under the guidance of my gurus, I chose to have my process accelerated. At times, I did not understand what was happening to me at all. I was afraid. Sometimes I felt like I had too much kundalini moving up through my body. It felt like glass shattering inside me.

Each trial (and there were many) was a test. Finally, I decided what I needed was solitude and silence. I went to Mallorca and rented a house near the beach. The very first night, my guru Shastriji appeared to me in a vision. He was in the back yard stirring up some "brew"—rice, dates, and what not. It was getting thicker and thicker, forming into a big patty. Then he sat on it and put all has *shakti* in it. Then he gave me a piece to eat—my *prassad* (holy food blessed by a saint or guru). Suddenly, I was out of control. I was flying high, I had no helmet, and there was no control panel in this jet. Then I woke up and I started writing.

Later, when I told Shastriji of my experience and I thanked him, he got that twinkle in his eye, and said, "By the grace of Babaji, I can go anywhere in the universe any time I want!" Then he snapped his fingers as if to say it was just a snap. Once again, I saw the result of all his years of devotion to Babaji and the Divine Mother and I was both humbled and in awe.

I do not pretend to have the full picture of the ultimate new paradigm for relationships. That would be ridiculous, as it is still emerging.

During all the years I taught the Loving Relationships Training, I was very careful to tell my students that I did not have all the answers. What I *did* have, was a lot of research and a lot of experience that was helpful. People appreciated that and still do. What I have always wanted was to be a catalyst; to stimulate new ideas. Of course, that is also my prayer here.

I assume that those of you who find this book are ready for change also . . . in your relationships and life, and I acknowledge you and appreciate it. I welcome you to the group of workers who are committed to this process. The community welcomes you; and we also welcome your ideas about this topic. I hope you will be stimulated to join us and to contribute to our research. I pray that you too will continue the work toward equanimity in relationships and peace on earth. I salute you and I would like to know you.

Love,

Sondra Ray

Part One:
Essays on
Relationships

UNEXPLORED TERRITORY

BECAUSE OF THE NATURE OF MY WORK, MY SPIRITUAL teachers have given me incredible *lilas* (divine strategy of the Master for cracking your case so that you may learn your lessons quickly). They have given me very intense training. Because it was my great privilege to be one of the first rebirthers on the planet, I was already a pioneer. So with all of this, and with all the research I had regarding how one's birth trauma affect's one's relationships, I was already beginning to study new paradigms. I never wrote about them specifically, but now I feel ready. This is an ongoing "process."

Recently I found myself exploring new fragrances, new brands of shampoo and toothpaste, new clothes, new places to go, new conversations, new feelings, new experiences. I was also in the mood for a new kind of relationship. If I were married now, would I be in trouble? Would I have to leave the marriage to find something new? Or could I co-create something new with a husband? If not, why not? I told myself that probably the reason I had not yet remarried was that I wanted to find a new paradigm, a new model, first. I was unwilling to go back to the old one, but was I stuck in transition? Where exactly was I with all these years of studying relationships, I asked myself.

When two souls come together they can easily get sucked into the old archetypes of relationships and marriage. I was really clear that I wanted to avoid that. I deliberately got involved with men who were different—who were also fed up with co-dependent symbiotic relationships. But exploring new mental arenas with them was scary and daring and I took risks that did not always work out. I found out that there was no right way to explore these new areas of relationship.

We all sense when an intimate relationship could be much more than we have made of it. But how many of us have truly begun the journey into this new territory? It is a decision that has to be made by both parties in the relationship—a decision to try this new adventure together.

In the past, marriage was a contract that represented physical survival. Some marriages were structured like trade agreements! Many couples today (at least in the West) believe that the relationship will satisfy his or her senses. A marriage or relationship where each partner seeks his or her own sense gratification only, is a union where each half has their own goal at the expense of a common purpose or goal. Each will only be happy with that relationship as it serves that person's own personal agenda. This makes it difficult for complete satisfaction as a couple.

Many people never question why they are together and what it all means or should mean. That is what this book is about: Why are you really together?

A SHOCKING REPORT

RESEARCHERS FROM THE HAZELTON CLINIC IN THE STATE of Minnesota reported, after studying the average American population, the following observations about the typical stages of relationships and how long those stages last.

1. The Dream Stage (Romance): Lasts up to two months.

2. The Disillusionment Stage: Lasts up to two years.

3. The Misery Stage: Can last up to thirty years!

4. The Enlightenment Stage: When the couple finally stops blaming each other and takes responsibility.

5. The Mutual Respect Stage

How do you feel about this? Isn't this enough to make you crave a new paradigm? It was for me! At first, I could not believe that someone would stay miserable for thirty years! But then I looked around and saw examples all around me of people who were doing just that. Maybe your own parents fit into that category. Maybe you fit into that category!

I also thought by the time a couple got to the enlightenment and mutual respect stage, they would be too old to enjoy it!

These are the reasons I got busy and created Loving Relationships Training, in the hope that we could jump from the Dream Stage to the Enlightenment Stage quickly, and save ourselves thirty years of misery.

Of course everyone would like to stay in the Dream

Stage forever; and some couples actually try to do just that. Instead they set themselves up for disappointment and disillusionment because of that old culprit, the unconscious. So isn't it better to be prepared? Isn't it better to know how your unconscious, negative thoughts affect your relationships, how your birth trauma affects your relationships, how your death urge and past lives affect your relationships? These are all parts of one's ego-based mentality. Who wants thirty years of misery? We have to learn how to get past these issues. This requires self analysis and spiritual work. We *can* use our relationships to help us achieve spiritual advancement, but we will need some new paradigms to do it.

Have you ever wondered why relationships don't turn out, or why you ended up divorced when you are a good person? The answer is that the ego says to seek love but never find it—or if you find it, get rid of it. To understand these concepts, we need knowledge: What is the ego? How do we deal with it? The ego represents our confusion about our identity. Without the ego, all would be love, and forever.

NEEDING A PARADIGM
OF BALANCE

MANY PEOPLE BELIEVE THE EVILS OF TODAY'S WORLD CAN be blamed on the six-thousand-year-old reign of patriarchal values as seen in warfare and competition and male domination. But it is too easy to blame the patriarchy alone. It is important to look at the effects of what we, both sexes, have co-created, in society. Should we not be working toward the end of *all* domination? After all, some men feel victimized by women!

One sex is not victimized by the other. THERE ARE NO VICTIMS. *A Course in Miracles* clearly teaches this: "There is nothing that happens without you calling for it, or asking for it."

Mary Daly, author of *Beyond God the Father*, points out that the model of the universe in which a male God rules the cosmos serves to legitimize male control of social institutions. She further states that, "The unconscious model continues to shape the perceptions even of those who have consciously rejected archaic religious teachings. The details of one's dogma are rejected, but the underlying structure of belief is imbedded at such a deep level it is rarely questioned" (Daly, 1985).

Therefore a system cannot simply be rejected, it must be *replaced*. We must *all* take responsibility for this and not blame men. In fact, many of us women could have been in past lives the very men who perpetuated this pattern! Scott Peck says, "We live in an oversexualized culture and undoubtedly the greatest burden of that is borne by women. Not simply as victims though. Men have been accused of treating women as sex objects . . . but women are the first to treat themselves that way . . . they are really out of kilter [in] the way they focus on their bodies. Women are held back by their own fear."

Many women feel that, in order to operate with any effectiveness in our culture, they have to immerse themselves in the values of male-dominated society. Many women do not trust their own truths because they grew up trying to please men. Feminism tried to address these issues but many women now feel unable to manage their spiritual paths and be in a loving relationship with a man. We must all face the fact that some of the above issues are causing pain in our relationships, in our families, and in society. That is the reason we must all think about it . . . without any blame.

If we are not in balance with the male and female sides of ourselves, we will experience conflict in our own minds. Resolution has to happen within first. But don't be surprised then if you attract fights with the opposite sex!

The power struggle is no fun. But there is a lot of confusion. Some women cannot stand feeling oppressed and powerless in a relationship. Other women may actually prefer an overpowering man. Some men feel their self esteem takes a blow living in the shadow of successful women. Other men are *only* attracted to strong, independent women! We *all* have to get our heads straight and give ourselves, and each other, time and space in which to do so.

DISCARDING OLD MODELS

IN ORDER FOR A NEW PARADIGM TO WORK, ONE HAS TO be willing to discard the outmoded models first. But what if we are attached or even addicted to those outmoded models? What if an outmoded model is something that one feels strongly about because of loyalty to one's parents or to one's culture? For example, men who have been given a model of masculinity they learned from their fathers might then mistrust any new model of maleness presented to them because of a sense of disloyalty. I once read an article in which family therapist Frank Pitman made this statement:

"Trying to teach a man with an outmoded model of masculinity to be an emotionally sensitive equal partner to a woman, is much like trying to teach a pig to sing!" (Pitman, 1994).

How depressing! I was glad a man wrote that! But it is not impossible to change.

Women have to face the fact that there are similar problems on the female side. If a woman does actually prefer an overpowering man, she will unconsciously then want to keep the old patriarchy intact. She probably won't see how this is hurting society, herself, or her children. Women are often afraid to become all they can be. It seems easier or more comfortable, in one sense, to give their power away to men and simply put up with old, outmoded styles. I assure you, this will not last—sooner or later they will get fed up!

It is no longer appropriate to maintain a patriarchal structure in our society; but that does not mean we want to return to a matriarchal system either. We must all commit to the end of resentment, destruction, and bad health—we must commit to the end of domination—period.

Here we are thus far: Both parties in a couple have to see the importance of new paradigms, they have to be equally willing to let go of old models, and they have to be committed to overthrowing generations of negative conditioning. This requires transformation. This requires doing the work of transformation on oneself. Spiritual work becomes the cornerstone for building the new paradigm together. It cannot be omitted. It has to be an integral part of one's daily life. It has to be a top priority.

I have already written fourteen books on the subject of clearing one's subconscious. I can recommend my own books, and especially the Loving Relationships Training and Rebirthing to start with.

RETHINKING HOW TO ATTRACT MATES

A TYPICAL PRIORITY LIST FOR ATTRACTING MATES GOES something like this:

1. There must be sexual chemistry.

2. We must share similar interests.

3. We must share similar religious backgrounds.

The spiritual masters recommend the reverse:

1. Soul unity is most important.

2. Sharing similar interests.

3. Sexual chemistry.

Notice that they did not leave out sexual attraction. It is definitely included. Soul unity is having similar spiritual goals and a willingness to achieve them, through discipline, alone or together, in a sweet way that works for both partners. This is absolutely vital in a relationship since one actually spends very little time having sex compared to the rest of one's life with a mate. The truth is we are attracted to another person because of the wave frequency of that person's soul. We must be totally aware of, and acknowledge, this fact.

Dion Fortune, in her book, *The Esoteric Philosophy of Love and Marriage*, states that couples connect in three different ways:

- through ordinary attractions of sex,

- by renewing karmic ties,

- according to Higher Cosmic Laws.

(Fortune, 1987)

The problem with using sexual attraction as the first priority is that one's judgment can be clouded or blinded by sex. Karmic ties are rooted in attractions experienced in past lives. The Cosmic Tie is the most profound and potent tie of all; something I would like to include in a new paradigm. The partnership is entered into by two individuals for the purpose of performing service. The partners offer themselves for service to the Master on the Inner Planes. They are mated with attention to their qualities and capacities—they do not choose each other. The Master chooses them. The pair opens a channel. Divine forces flow through them with astounding power, magnetizing them and their surroundings. Through this union, the power of each partner is augmented; and they are brought to their highest level of perfection.

Dion Fortune also talks about the importance of mating on matching planes.

1. The Physical and Material

2. The Lower Astral

3. The Upper Astral

4. The Lower Mental

5. The Upper Mental

6. The Lower Spiritual

7. The Upper Spiritual

For example, if a man who has three developed planes marries a woman who has only two functioning planes, psychic and spiritual disaster can occur. The union of equals is ideal. According to Fortune, unless we mate on each one of our planes, our union will be incomplete.

KNOWING WHAT YOU WANT
FROM A RELATIONSHIP

I HAVE READ THAT RESEARCHERS FROM THE UNIVERSITY of Arizona found that the secret to lasting love was that couples shared a similar vision of the relationship. This is obvious in one sense, but how many people really discuss what it is they want from a relationship? What do you want?

1. Do you want comfort and security? (Does that mean you think the boat should never be rocked?)

2. Are you looking for economic security? (Does that mean you think you cannot make it on your own?)

3. Are you looking for sensual satisfaction? (What happens if your sex life isn't satisfactory . . . is that time for divorce then?)

4. Are you looking for a business partnership? (If so, you better tell the truth and remember that limited motives, such as sex and money, won't be satisfying.)

5. Are you looking for companionship? (Does it mean you are afraid of being alone? Or you cannot stand living alone? How can anyone else live with you if you cannot live with yourself?)

6. Do you think the purpose of life is to get married, have kids, and then die? (Have you never questioned traditional assumptions about life and relationships? Do you know what you want from life, yourself?)

What if you said that what you wanted from a relationship was that which was the highest for you, that which was really good for you? And what if what was really good for you was this: To have all your dark shadows revealed and removed.

Of course, we all want our relationships to help us discover what life is like at its best. Who doesn't want that? But your dark shadows have to be removed before you can discover that. Having a mate as a mirror is a powerful way to recognize them. A relationship is a test of all your spiritual qualities. Surrender to the fact that your mate is your guru and your relationship is the best seminar you can ever take. That is the right attitude. Your partner will reflect all your patterns. Your relationship is an educational process. Therefore, you better talk about your expectations early in the game—the sooner the better! From a spiritual point of view, your relationship will be a success if it is dedicated to truth, and determined by a *vision of truth*.

You and your mate have to make your own map. You should not assume that your purposes are aligned simply because you have common interests. I don't think it is good to wait until after your first sexual experience together to discuss your intentions either. Your ability to discriminate as regards what long-range qualities are needed in a committed relationship may be thrown off center. Knowing when you can talk about such deep subjects is the tricky part. It takes positive self esteem to bring up these issues early.

STEP ONE IN THE PARADIGM: KNOWING THE PURPOSE OF LIFE

I READ ONCE THAT ROBIN WILLIAMS' MOTHER TOLD HIM as a child that the purpose of life was to experience intense joy! (Imagine having a mother like that!) My gurus in India believe that the purpose of life is to recognize the Supreme. They understand that we are here to learn to recognize ourselves and others as part of the Supreme God. Knowing who you really are leads to intense joy.

A third purpose in life is to learn. Our world is a school and we must never stop being students in it. Learning includes changing, and expanding.

A fourth purpose in life is to clear your karma. If you want to know more about that subject read books like *We Were Born Again to be Together*, by Dick Sutphen, and *Other Lives, Other Selves*, by Dr. Roger Woolger.

Ram Dass once said, "You are here to Take the Curriculum." Use your "case" (i.e., your particular issues, karmas, etc.) as a stepping stone.

A fifth purpose in life is to serve humanity. This is, and always will be, considered the first and foremost duty of the mature soul. This is called Karma Yoga.

A sixth purpose in life is the dissolution of the ego. This is a step-by-step process of giving up separation and limitation which leads to the experience of ourselves as Divine Masters. This, in turn, leads to permanent liberation in which one transcends the human condition. One achieves permanent status in the Absolute.

In life, we experience a continuous push toward egolessness. A being has an intense desire to know its real self, to know the truth, the Eternal Source. Our overriding desire is to discover this source of infinite love and to express this love in daily life.

The purpose of the relationship is to enhance these goals. Both partners must share this intention or they are missing the boat and they will just have to keep dying and reincarnating until they get it!

Everyone is a potential candidate for total enlightenment; everyone has the blueprint. That is why we are here. Read *A Course in Miracles* (see Bibliography) for the most profound teachings of all on this subject. These books are the most important works in two thousand years.

Just today I opened the Course at random to page 331. Here is what I saw first: "In the unholy relationship it is not the body of the other with which union is attempted, but the bodies of those who are not there!" In other words, we are attracted to and addicted to the positive aspects, and especially the negative aspects, of our caretakers from childhood. We have to work this out. It is our curriculum, our assignment, to get unstuck from the past. However, the ego cannot tolerate release from the past. Therefore you are left with having to deal with ego. That is why *A Course in Miracles* is a required course. We all have to deal with our egos sooner or later. If we wait, we are only dragging out the pain and delaying our own happiness. Is your purpose happiness? Then Realization of God must be your primary desire.

BEING WITH AN EQUAL

IMAGINE THIS: MEN AND WOMEN AS FULL PARTNERS IN running society. It is going to happen. In fact, the partnership has already been set in motion. Why not get with the program now? Why not be a part of this exciting idea?

Do you fear having an equal? Begin to process the truth by answering these questions:

MEN

1. Are you afraid of giving up control?

2. Are you afraid of being out of control?

3. Are you afraid that if you are not in control, she would be?

4. Are you afraid of someone standing up to you? Are you afraid of feedback?

5. Are you afraid of facing yourself?

6. Are you afraid she will become your mother?

7. Are you afraid you won't be able to do what you want if you don't make all the final decisions?

8. Are you afraid of being disloyal to your father's patterns?

9. Are you afraid of change in yourself?

10. Are you afraid of the energy, the synergy, the possible excitement of creativity?

What ARE you afraid of?

WOMEN

1. Are you afraid of your own power, of standing out?

2. Are you afraid you'll be lost without someone controlling you?

3. Are you afraid to stand up to a man and be yourself?

4. Are you afraid of your real self?

5. Are you afraid you cannot make it on your own so it is better to put up with being controlled than being alone?

6. Are you afraid of being different than your mother?

7. Are you afraid you cannot do it anyway? You are not as good as a man?

8. Are you afraid people will criticize you if you rock the boat?

9. Are you afraid you won't be able to keep the peace unless you give your power away and give in?

10. Are you afraid of the energy, the excitement, the aliveness of it all?

What ARE you afraid of?

It is our job to give up and get over our fears. Accepting this responsibility is part of becoming enlightened. It is absolutely mandatory that you have worked out methods of clearing, because if you find an equal, the first thing you will have to deal with is a lot of energy. This energy between equals is very intense—just the sheer *life* of it will bring up anything unlike itself. So you will have to understand conflict resolution and you will need to know how to handle your unconscious. Equal partnership can be fun—if you both agree to it and if you both know spiritual purification techniques.

Don't deprive yourself of the excitement of having an equal!

THE INTERVIEW

BECAUSE OF MY CONSTANT TRAVELING DUE TO THE nature of my work, I have often risked not bothering to get enough information about a man before I got involved with him. I just went with the flow, which was spontaneous and fun in one sense, but often resulted in disasters later. (I lived with one man for only one day!)

I decided to get smart. I started to question new male acquaintances: "How do you feel about God?" and, "How do you feel about living forever?" I dared ask these questions very early in the relationship. Their answers told me a lot about them. I thought my powers of discrimination were improving. I started meeting men who seemed very spiritual and who said they wanted to be Immortal. But they were not willing to act on their beliefs. They were, in fact, threatened by change, threatened by processing, and—worst of all—threatened by me! Since then, I have had to rethink and refine my approach. You have to know yourself, and not be afraid to "put it out there." It takes a high level of self esteem to risk exposing yourself, but it is worth it. Why fall madly in love with someone who just does not have the visions or goals that you have?

You can begin interviewing a potential equal by finding out about his or her "relationship history." This usually reveals itself spontaneously. If it does not, make a conscious effort to uncover this information early in the relationship—as part of the getting-to-know-you stage. After that, if you are still interested, proceed with questions such as those below. (By the way, you don't have to ask them all in one night!)

1. What is your vision of the purpose of a relationship?

2. What are your top priorities in life?

3. Tell me how you feel about God? Goddess?

4. Tell me how you feel about living forever?

5. Are you willing to strive for total enlightenment? If yes, does that mean you are willing to do whatever it takes, such as by processing or spiritual purifications?

6. What is your method of problem solving? Do you retreat? Do you communicate?

7. What are your issues about money? About food? (If you are a vegetarian, you'd better talk about it —and a lot more. . .)

This may sound calculating and unromantic . . . but if you avoid asking about issues that are important to you, you will probably regret it.

Try your interview in a romantic setting. Most importantly, always be aware of the danger that they may unconsciously try to please you and say what they think you want to hear. (You might do the same when they interview you!). In either case, answering without integrity will backfire later. We—you and I—*know* this to be true!

•

A SACRED PARTNERSHIP

•

To live by the underlying principle of a new paradigm—that each partner is equally committed in assisting the other in his or her spiritual growth. Each must understand that the most profound reason they are together is for the evolution of their souls. This creates a whole new vibration between the couple.

A relationship should be about growth and movement. It should create a holy, interpersonal environment for the evolution of two souls. A relationship is a process; in that process, the couple should celebrate changes in themselves which are stimulated by one another. They should not resent the fact that the mate (the relationship) is encouraging them to change. Each should want the other to become all that he or she can be, and should not feel threatened by this desire. In other words, you should not hold yourself back in any way, nor should you allow the other to hold you back. In fact, you should use the support of your mate to help propel you forward, to advance. Each should enjoy empowering the other, but neither should give away his or her power. Don't sell out—work it out!

I am describing intimacy as a path. Strive for intimacy instead of intensity because intimacy leads to transformation. The power of intimacy brings up all of one's fears to be processed. You must first want to become enlightened so you can make the relationship work for you. Then you must eliminate all barriers to expressing your love.

Beware of using a special relationship as a substitute for God. This is most important to understand. *A Course in Miracles* says that "A special relationship is the ego's chief weapon to keep you from God" (Foundation for Inner Peace, 1991). So, if you are spending all your time and energy (as most people do) trying to make a relationship work with someone who you think is more special than you or anyone else, it will never work.[1]

In the new paradigm, we must have a mystical purpose that transcends the personal needs of the two people in the relationship. This requires a partner who is willing to work with you on forming a triangle with God. That is why I suggest you spend some time interviewing a person before you have sex with them. So what if the "interview" takes nine months? It has been recommended by the masters that you wait nine months before having sex anyway, if you really want your relationship to work. Otherwise you could be in grave danger of being led down the wrong road without even realizing it. Sex brings up everything and often too fast.

I am talking about a paradigm where two partners are striving for the spiritual adventure of exploring the higher possibilities of Spirit together. Ask yourself, are you willing to go for it?[2]

Endnote

1. See "The Tyranny of a Special Relationship" in *A Course in Miracles*.

2. I recommend Zukav's book, *Seat of the Soul*.

HAVING A SPIRITUAL
MISSION TOGETHER

IMAGINE WHAT WOULD HAPPEN IF A COUPLE SAT DOWN and decided, right from the beginning, what kind of mission they were going to accomplish together for the world—*and then actually did it!* This spiritual mission could be a joint career. If they were already in different careers, they could still decide what kind of service they could offer the world together apart from their careers.

When people are deeply in love, they feel a natural concern for the state of the world and they want to do something about it. If love has waned and the relationship is stale, it might just be because the couple never acted on that sense of purpose. It is never too late to infuse your marriage or relationship with this gift. It is not only a gift to the world, but a gift to the relationship; it gives the relationship true meaning.

I have studied successful relationships of partners who were equally powerful. In fact, the equality in the relationship was part of the success. Bill and Hillary Clinton are a good example. They shared their commitment to public service before Bill became Governor of Arkansas. It is clear that this unity of purpose has helped them weather the storms of their marital life. They were focused on something greater than themselves. I think the American public has forgiven them their marital troubles because *everyone* has a past, and who wants a leader untempered by life's lessons? Most importantly, I think we wanted to take the chance and experiment with equals running our country together. This is the new paradigm.

I read an article recently called "100 Ways to Fix the World." The author interviewed one hundred famous people and asked them their recommendations. Filmmaker Eleanor Coppola said, "Every seven years, every able body should do three months of public service." This is a really good idea—for everyone! If you are single, you might meet the man or woman of your dreams while doing it.

Missions are satisfying. In my case, finding mine felt like the beginning of my true life. Everything before that was peanuts; I consider it like a past life. When I tell people what I was doing before I accepted and carried out my mission, they cannot believe I am the same person.

Once I held a class wherein each student selected a mission and then shared with the class what he or she had chosen. Almost everyone totally underestimated their abilities—it was shocking! Choose something way beyond what you think you can do. This is called a "big stretch." Big stretches make you expand and, at the same time, they heal you. In my case, I needed help with relationships. I looked around, but in those days there were almost no seminars on relationships at all—not even in California! So I said, "Well, somebody has to study this . . . somebody should be teaching this—I guess it has to be me!" And that was how I first stretched to find my mission to become the founder of a huge international organization, Loving Relationships Training, which continued for nearly twenty years before I accepted my new mission.

LOVING YOURSELF HELPS
YOU TO LOVE ANOTHER

To stay loving with one another we must stay loving with ourselves. Often, when we first come out of victim consciousness and try to take responsibility for everything we have created, we forget to do this in a self-loving manner. We know that the old way of blaming others for our problems is no longer applicable, but we must also be careful not to turn everything into self-blame. This tendency will add negative mental mass (self-pity, guilt, shame, etc.) to the situation, making it harder to give up the problem.

Feeling shame and guilt for our mistakes is just another form of self-punishment. Many of us have left religions that perpetrated this kind of approach to growth. We must be careful not to re-create this same structure within our new paradigms; otherwise we are in danger of re-inventing the very patriarchal religions we've run away from.

I know one man who had to go to bed for two whole weeks when he realized that it was he himself who had created everything in his life. Taking responsibility for our life should not result in guilt such as his. The point here is to realize the benefit you now have in the future, to create life just the way you want it and to realize your creative power to manifest happiness from now on! Forgive yourself for the past. When you make a mistake, notice the thoughts that created the mistake, let them go and attempt to do better next time. In other words, keep the self-love intact no matter what.

It takes time and commitment to learn how to make this paradigm work. In the beginning, it might take awhile to figure out what thoughts created the problem, but with practice, this awareness will happen more quickly. Acquiring the right "tools," and then learning to use them in the process is important. Rebirthing is one of these tools. It is well worth your while to understand the rebirthing process and find the right rebirther. Once you have integrated rebirthing, you will be able to unravel your mistakes a lot faster and thereby minimize the need for damage control.

The ability to love ourselves even when we make mistakes is important, for it is an aspect of our feminine side or the Divine Mother energy within each of us. You still love a child when he or she makes a mistake. Can you not also love yourself in the same way? If you do, you will make fewer mistakes in the future. When you start judging yourself, you get nervous and things get worse. Also, if you stop loving yourself, others might stop loving you too; then you will feel even more unsteady. It helps to remember that everyone makes mistakes. Mistakes help you grow. Two people who love themselves as well as one another, and who take appropriate responsibility for their personal realities, can come together as a couple in a whole new way to create a new paradigm.

GOING FOR TOTAL
ENLIGHTENMENT

THERE ARE MANY DIFFERENT DEFINITIONS OF ENLIGHT-
enment. Any new paradigm for a relationship should
emphasize the importance of agreement and commitment
by both partners as they reach their own definitions.

Leonard Orr, founder of Rebirthing, used to define
enlightenment as "Certain Knowledge of the Absolute
Truth" (i.e., knowing and remembering that your thoughts
create your results). If one person in a relationship accepts
this, but the other is not willing to consider the fact that
his or her negative thoughts are producing negative results,
how can the relationship work? The Bible says, "As a man
thinketh, so is he" and, "Thou art ensnared by the words
of thy mouth."

An enlightened couple will constantly evaluate the
results they get and study what thoughts and words
brought about those results. They will evaluate what
thoughts they need to change and they will both work
diligently on changing them.

A Course in Miracles defines enlightenment as choosing
the Holy Spirit's thought system instead of the Ego's
thought system. An enlightened couple knows the difference and is vigilant against the ego. The ego is based on
separation; the result is guilt, separation, fear, pain, struggle, misery, suffering, anger, depression, sickness, and
death. The enlightened couple constantly works toward
eliminating limited negative thoughts that lead to those
ego states. Instead, they choose thoughts that are in keeping with the Holy Spirit's reality (i.e. union, life, love, joy,
peace, harmony, health). The enlightened couple also

knows that minds are joined and that each is a reflection of the other.

If you are operating in an enlightened paradigm, you will also understand and honor the following statements and how each applies to your relationship (also from the Course):

> *You will attack what does not satisfy you to avoid seeing you created it.*
>
> *Beware of the temptation to perceive yourself as unjustly treated.*
>
> *Only I can deprive myself of anything.*
>
> *There is nothing that happens without my calling for it or asking for it.*

In other words: "Life presents to me what my thoughts are." This also means, of course, that blaming is off the track. In other words: "I am responsible for what I see, I choose the feelings I experience and everything that happens to me I have asked for."

Being enlightened has to do with taking responsibility for all the results in your life all the time. The Course will tell you that all trials are lessons you failed to learn before; you are always given another chance to choose again and do better.

The source of all of our experience is the mind. We rule and direct our minds and consequently, we must change our thoughts to restore our mind to its full potential.

THE WILLINGNESS TO CLEAR:
SELF-ANALYSIS

NEW AGE COUPLES WHO ARE ENLIGHTENED HAVE SIMI-lar problems to everyone else; however, they attempt to apply the self-realization techniques to their relationship. These couples try to break old, destructive patterns in their relationships and try to create new, healthy models or paradigms. They know that their relationship is central to their spiritual path and they are committed to doing whatever it takes to stay on track.

I see some couples in which one partner is willing to practice self-analysis and the other is not. This combination rarely works. The partner willing to process usually starts to grow a lot faster than the other and it becomes obvious that they do not share similar levels of commit-ment to that path. If you find yourself in a relationship like this, you need to look at why you created this situa-tion for yourself—and if it is right to stay.

The spiritual master, Yogananda, has always said that self-analysis is the key to the mastery of life. He has also stated that, without self-analysis, man leads a robot-like life:

> People who never analyze themselves are like mechanical products of the factory of their envi-ronment. They are preoccupied with breakfast, lunch, and dinner, working and sleeping, and being entertained. They don't know what or why they are seeking, nor why they never realize com-plete happiness. (Yogananda, 1982).

The Bible says, "Be perfect even as God is perfect." That is an assignment. The only way to have a perfect rela-tionship is if both people are willing to experience their perfection. To experience your own perfection you must release the ego's thought system. And, in a relationship, you both have to be committed to this. Appropriate self-analysis is essential. If there is resistance to self-analysis, find out why. Of course, that too requires self-analysis!

One must also take the necessary steps to clear the old negative thoughts out of the body. This requires some kind of spiritual purification such as rebirthing, chanting, relationships trainings. One hazard for couples to watch for is the tendency to use activities, such as meditating together, as an avoidance technique. That is why I prefer rebirthing. It is active clearing and your rebirther won't let you get away with avoidance. Another hazard is *over processing* with your mate, processing which is too serious and work-oriented. This approach defeats the purpose. Processing can be fun and if you are willing, you can have more fun for the rest of your life. (You will never find this out, however, until you *do it* and keep it up!)

Self-analysis can be as simple as processing on a piece of paper:

1. My thoughts which created this situation are:

2. The desired result outcome of this situation is:

3. The new thoughts or affirmations I need to think about in order to achieve this desired outcome are:

HANDLING KARMIC
DEBTS AND DUES

ONE OF THE REASONS SELF-ANALYSIS AND PROCESSING
are underestimated is that people are often not aware of
the laws of reincarnation and karma. An understanding
of these laws contributes immeasurably to the process of
clearing. These laws are an integral part of the Rebirthing
community's paradigms.

The spiritual master Yogananda says, "Reincarnation
is the progress of a soul through many lives on the earth
plane, as through so many grades in a school, before it
'graduates' to the immortal perfection of oneness with
God." He also says that in order to comprehend the justi-
fication of man's seeming inequalities, we must first
understand the law of reincarnation. Knowledge of this
law was lost in the West during the Dark Ages. Yogananda
says Jesus spoke of this law when he said, "Elias is come
already; and they knew him not." (Elias reincarnated as
John the Baptist.) Yogananda points out that, without
reincarnation, there would be no divine justice operating
for those souls who have not yet had a chance to express
themselves, such as a baby born dead (Yogananda, 1982).

If there were no law of cause and effect in the physical
world, all would be chaos. Meher Baba says:

> All that has happened in past lives does have its
> own unconscious, but effective, share in deter-
> mining one's actions and responses in this life.
> Fate is really man's own creation pursuing him
> from past lives. Karmic determination is the con-
> dition of true responsibility. It means that an
> individual will reap what he sows. According to

Karmic Law he can neither avoid the debts or the dues. It is through his own binding karma that he invites upon himself pleasure or pain. He keeps reincarnating to pay off his debts and recover his dues. But even then he may be unable to clear his account for two reasons: 1) All the persons with whom he or she has karmic links may not be incarnate when he has taken a body. 2) Due to particular limitations of his capacities or circumstances, he or she may not be able to meet all the complex circumstances. He may even go on adding to his debts or dues (i.e., creating NEW karma!). The result could be that there is difficulty getting out of his complex karmic entanglements. These entanglements would be endless if there were no provisions for release. The help of a Perfect Master is enormous for this. The Perfect Master can bring emancipation. Another way out is spiritual purification and service to humanity" (*Discourses*, pp. 334-337).

It is very important to become conscious of the concepts of reincarnation and karma so that you may have a deeper understanding of what is going on in your life, yourself, and in your relationships with others. If you meet someone new and you feel instantly repulsed by him or her, perhaps you share some bad karma. If you meet someone and you experience instant camaraderie, perhaps you have shared good past lives with this person. The same dynamic holds true for entire countries. What parts of the world have you always wanted to visit? Are there other places you would *never* travel to? Clear it. Go!

THE GOAL OF
STABILIZATION OF BLISS

HOW OFTEN HAVE YOU, AS PART OF A COUPLE, HAD THE experience of true bliss together, and wanted to stay there, but just could not? Something happened and you came crashing down. It was a devastating feeling. You long to go back to bliss. Is this not one of the reasons we might become so addicted to sex? Sex gives us but a momentary experience of what *samadhi* is like.

We don't have a lot of experience with Bliss Consciousness. If you try to imagine a paradigm of a couple in bliss most of the time you may find it difficult, if not impossible. We have no reality to back up this idea as a real possibility. We tend to use the past as a reference point. We have experienced very few such points of being able to stay in bliss with another person, or even alone. Because of these past experiences, we end up with the subconscious thought, "If I am in bliss now, something terrible will happen later." (I will fall out of bliss.) We become scared of this feeling and the fear pushes bliss farther away—yet we still long for it! You have to look at why this is: "Love [bliss] brings up anything unlike itself." In other words, the bliss of love will bring up the opposite, which is the ego. Bliss, like love, "triggers" ego material that needs to be processed. (Is that not why great sex drives people nuts?)

You should not give up your intention of having bliss. What you intend, you become. Every time you have a bliss experience and crash afterwards, it simply means that more of your ego has been processed—it does not mean it is impossible to keep your bliss. So long as you stay on the path to total enlightenment, eventually your periods of bliss will be longer and the crashes will become shorter and less painful. Most spiritual masters who are in bliss all the time worked very hard to get there. It is a process of unraveling the mind, and it is a long process.

In Meher Baba's profound book, *Discourses*, he carefully explains the stages of the Path. There are seven stages of advancement before the soul gets to Permanent Bliss, or total annihilation of the ego (a humbling process!). This chapter has greatly increased my respect for the true spiritual path.

One of the reasons I go to the Himalayas every single year is so that I can experience (and vibrate toward) those saints who are constantly in bliss. I need a reality check. I need to know it is possible. I have no framework or model for bliss elsewhere in my life.

In spiritual life, this is called the *principle of right association* or putting yourself in contact with the highest, most blissful people possible for as long as you can stand it. You are forced to adapt upward! (In other words, be careful who you hang out with. You might be tempted to match energies with low vibrations.)

THE IMMORTAL COUPLE
AS A NEW PARADIGM

INSTEAD OF GETTING OLD TOGETHER AND DYING, imagine the opposite. What if both of you could become ageless as a couple, and live as long as you wanted to together—even hundreds of years! Sounds farfetched? Not anymore it is not. We now have the knowledge to make this happen. Dr. Depak Chopra is writing and lecturing on the subject of physical immortality and backing it up scientifically.

An immortal is a soul who has already taken on enough male and female incarnations that the birth/ death cycle can now be transcended; he or she can stay here to serve as long as he or she chooses. (See backlist books.)

In order for a couple to become immortal, they obviously have to work out their "unconscious death urge." This is an incredible subject for a couple to study together. You have to master the philosophy, psychology, and physiology of the unconscious.

What this does for a relationship is simply incredible. The relationship takes on a whole new vibration of sheer vitality. The sacredness increases also because life is God; and so more life equals more holiness! When two immortals are together, there is a sense of well-being that pervades the underlying structure of the relationship. I have seen relationships in which each person is constantly dealing with the suppression of fear such as when is this other person going to leave or die? Also, a typical couple usually projects the unconscious death urge onto the relationship: The tendency is to kill it off in insidious ways.

Many people cannot stand the idea of physical immortality because it is too exciting! They might be addicted to the pain and struggle. Others simply do not want to live forever in a physical body because they hate their life! (They do not know that one of the reasons their life does not work is because they have not cleared their death urge.) "Death is a result of the thought called the ego, just as surely as life is a result of the thought called God" (Foundation for Inner Peace, 1992). Understanding this point is imperative.

When a couple strives for this expression of the Divine, they each become strong and healthy; there is a miraculous and free flow of psychic energy. This energy can then be channeled into meaningful self-expression. When a couple expresses together the glory of immortality into their life and society, they function as effective instruments for creative action and a realization of higher values in the world.[1] They truly discover what life is at its best and they are willing and happy to share their blossoming emotional and sexual relationship.

Endnote

1. For more information on immortality, read *How to be Chic, Fabulous, and Live Forever*, also published by Celestial Arts.

REBIRTHING AS A WAY OF LIFE
IN THE NEW PARADIGM

IMAGINE INSTALLING A WONDERFUL JACUZZI OR HOT TUB in your bedroom, living room, or outside. As a daily routine, a couple (or even the whole family) soaks together and rebirth each other instead of arguing. During the rebirthing, they let go of tension, pain, and disease-producing stress. They channel new ideas for their business or future. They get clear on potential relationship problems. Does this scenario sound farfetched? It isn't. There are thousands of rebirthers already living like this right now.

"But I am not a rebirther," you say. Well, we can teach you—and easily. Imagine the fun of having other friends come over and share this experience with you as an alternative to watching television or going bowling! Imagine helping each other openly with the deep problems that everyone experiences (even if they pretend they don't). The Rebirthing community is supportive. We get high together on love and air. You can too. Rebirthing is becoming a way of life in many places.

At the beginning of a relationship, we recommend that each member of the couple get rebirthed by a skilled rebirther outside of the relationship until they work through the majority of the birth trauma and unconscious death urge. Later, the rebirther will train you how to rebirth yourselves. The next step is to learn how to rebirth others.

This new paradigm is catching on already. We have spent two decades perfecting these trainings. It won't be long before this is natural and desirable by all. (Many people have not heard about it yet, but they will. And if they hear about it, *and* try it, I am convinced they will then get as excited as we have been for years about this technique.) Rebirthing can save your life and it can save your relationships. If that were not so, I would not have dropped everything and dedicated my whole life to the teaching of it.

Imagine this scene: You are tired, cranky—you have a migraine. You don't even want to see your mate. You cannot be bothered. You feel overwhelmed by the kids. You want to give up. Your mate becomes furious; it gets worse. It takes a week to recover from this upset. You feel a headache coming on. You tell your mate you need to go into the rebirthing room and the hot tub. He comes in and assists you. You discover the thoughts you have that are causing this possible migraine. You breathe them out. You feel fantastic after only twenty minutes. If this sounds like an appealing alternative to your current circumstances, why not join us for an easier life?

PROBLEM SOLVING IN
THE NEW PARADIGM

PERHAPS YOU ARE THINKING, "REBIRTHING SOUNDS great, but what if I cannot afford a jacuzzi, or what if I am somewhere else where there is no hot tub?" Well, good question. You could then do a dry rebirthing. (Rebirthers have even had spontaneous rebirths on planes, in restaurants, and even in church.) But let's be practical. What if you need to settle a problem right now and rebirthing is not appropriate or you are not interested in learning it?

In the new paradigm, a person who is committed to truth believes in telling the complete truth *faster* (and has more fun as a result). It is important for couples to establish methods and rules for problem solving, methods that you both like and can honor. It is important that you agree to reserve the right to remind your partner of these methods. Two of the most helpful problem solving processes are: Creating the right state of mind and learning how to be an active listener.

State of Mind

1. Remember that you and your mate or partner in business are on the same side wanting to solve the problem together.

2. Remember that the goal is to go for the solution, not to drag out a debate where someone wins and someone loses.

3. Remember that you can disagree without upsetting each other.

4. Remember that there is a way to prevent an argument, but you both have to be willing to play the game of going for the highest spiritual thought.

5. Remember that using anger (as a way of manipulating, controlling, or getting what you want) is not enlightened. The goal is always to be as enlightened as possible.

6. To get what you want, you have to ask for it. If the other person does not want what you want, then you have the choice of negotiating a compromise until each of you sees the intrinsic value for each of you, together or separately.

7. Find out which points you can agree on and acknowledge those which help to relax you, such as, "I agree that you deserve to have more time to yourself . . . but how can we also get enough time for the children?"

Active Listening

1. Sit down and face each other and look into each other's eyes. One of you begins to share and the other simply listens without interruption. A timer can be used so that each person has ten minutes or so to talk uninterrupted. If you are the listener you should *not* be rehearsing what you are going to say. In fact, you should listen well enough that you can actually report back what has been said: You might say, "The main thing I think you are saying to me is that you really feel hurt by what I did at the party last night." The listener does not defend or explain anything. You only summarize what you heard to make sure your understanding is accurate.

2. If you are the person doing the communicating and you feel that the listener did not understand something, then you must repeat it until it can be repeated back. Good communication is up to the communicator.

3. *Listen* to what is said. Ask yourself what it is you need or want to hear. Learn about where you need to improve your listening habits.

4. When the communicator feels that he or she was actually heard properly, then you can switch roles.

It is important to remember that all sharing be done without blame. Also, each party must be willing to look at how they've helped to create the upset. This is key in an enlightened paradigm. When both people take responsibility, healing happens!

My Australian acupuncturist, Vicki Wooler, has this sign on her wall:

IS THIS A PROBLEM, OR AN
OPPORTUNITY TO LEARN?

CONFLICT RESOLUTION

SOMETIMES WE CAN'T ALWAYS BE IN AGREEMENT WITH each other, but we must be able to disagree and still love. Paul Ferrini, in his book *Love Without Conditions—Reflections of the Christ Mind*, talks about basing love on the notion of agreement. Constantly seeking agreement can lead to the ultimate co-dependency trip. I *can* disagree with you and you can disagree with me and we do not have to get upset —that is the main point behind the following technique:

When each person takes a very different position on a potential decision that has to be made, use the game of "Going to the Highest Spiritual Thought." This is an alternative to arguing or having one person end up feeling like they have to give in to the other. The couple must be totally committed to finding a solution as fast as possible; solution must be more important than wanting to argue, be right, win, or control. The couple must remember that they are on the same team; they are not in competition with each other. I call this the game of finding the highest spiritual thought. I chanelled this game after much prayer.

The Highest Spiritual Thought is always the thought that is the most loving, the least limiting, the most productive for both, and feels the best in your body. It is the most positive thought. A kind of relief will take over in your energy field when it arises. An example:

A couple is on the verge of an argument about how to spend the evening. She wants to go to the opera and he wants to go to the movies. Instead of fighting, they simply look at the alternatives to find out which feels like the highest thought.

a. He could go to the opera with her tonight and she could go to the movie with him tomorrow night.

b. They could go alone—she to the opera, he to the movies.

c. They could do something completely different, like go to a spa.

The only drawback to this game is when people refuse to play it because some people are actually addicted to conflict. Both people must begin by dropping their "positions," or differences completely. Chances are great that the highest spiritual thought will end up being better than either position!

One person puts out the highest thought he or she can think of about the issue. The other then puts out one that might be higher. They go back and forth until they reach the "highest thought." If my boyfriend, for example, put out higher thought, then I would gladly leave mine and go up to his. And vice versa. We want the best outcome for all concerned.

If there seems to be difficulty in discerning which of the two thoughts is absolutely the highest, do not debate it. Agree to part for awhile and meditate.

•

BLESSING INSTEAD OF JUDGING

•

ALTHOUGH BLESSING INSTEAD OF JUDGING IS AN ANCIENT
practice, it might be new for you to develop the habit of
blessing those whom you want to judge.

The *kahunas* of Hawaii teach that even mentally criti-
cizing others affects your body. They teach that criticism
of the self or of others causes stress and inhibits awareness, memory, and energy flow, making you weaker and
more susceptible to illness.

The Bible teaches us that someone who is thankful
for all things will be made glorious and that attitudes of
love, praise, and gratitude fill one with an incomprehensi-
ble power of the Spirit. These are called the "ascension
attitudes."

We may know these ideas, but applying them at all
times is another story. When someone displays a behavior
that is intolerable, we usually don't feel like praising them
for it. To break the habit of judging that person, try blessing the situation instead. Support the person in moving
through the offensive pattern, bless them, see them as
healed of it, and honor and respect their God Self. This is
easier to do if the relationship is already placed in the
context of conscious blessing.

Blessing what you want *daily* and focusing on *praise* as a
habit will create a safe space in your relationship. A sense
of peace and relaxation should be the context of any relationship; and this should be re-established daily—tele-
pathically, and verbally. If a couple makes a point of
focusing on praise as a daily discipline, preferably in a
sacred space (such as before an altar), then everything that
happens is placed in that context. When that context is

CREATING
SACRED
RELATIONSHIPS

repeatedly re-established, each partner becomes more willing to resolve issues and work out his or her own dark shadows with the support and encouragement of the other. If your mate knows, with certainty, that you continually bless him and do not judge his true being or self, he will not be threatened by discussion of those actions or habits that need to be corrected in order for him to become totally enlightened.

However, if someone has come from a home where criticism and verbal abuse was common, he may not only expect criticism, but may try to draw that same behavior out of his mate. The mind seeks familiarity. He may unconsciously want criticism and judgment so that he will "feel at home." Or he may want it so that he can feel the familiar resentment. Praise and gratitude might even seem suspicious to a mind addicted to criticism. This self-induced pattern is an obstacle that must be overcome. Enlightened couples must become aware of this obstacle and deal with it together.

Start by blessing everything and by practicing *praise saturation.*

Blessing Situations

Let's say you find yourself in a place you do not like from which there is no escape. You feel like complaining. Instead, ask yourself, "What is my good purpose for having created this situation? What can I learn from it?" Then ask yourself, "How can I lift the resonance here?" The answer is to bless the place and the situation as your teacher and to bless it as valuable even though it may not have met your standard of quality and beauty. You may actually bring about a change there. You can also bless everyone and everything that represents what you want. Creating verbal blessings is a way to express gratitude, create powerful affirmations, and take responsibility for shifting negative energy.

Praise Saturation

Many people have no idea how great they are. Perhaps they have had tons of parental disapproval. They may be starved for acknowledgment. Praise saturation merely means you acknowledge them verbally in every way you can think of—and you do it sincerely, finding those qualities that are really great and true in that person.

Praise saturation can be done formally or informally. In a formal approach you would seat the person before a group. Each member or "praiser" in the group tells this person something they like and appreciate about him or her. Continue until a saturation point is reached (as long as you feel it is right). Say whatever truthful thought comes to mind:

> "Something I really like about you is your upbeat attitude and positive energy."

> "Something else I really like about you is your passion for life."

> "Something else wonderful about you is your ability to stay calm and focused in a crisis."

Informally, you can do this anytime and anywhere with anyone. Make sure the person hears these acknowledgments. When a family member accomplishes something good, it is very important to acknowledge and bless them so they can reinforce the manifestation of this good quality. Try it.

GIVING AND RECEIVING
FEEDBACK IN THE
NEW PARADIGM

FEEDBACK IS A DELICATE AND CHALLENGING TOPIC. Enlightened beings who are clear that their goal is total illumination usually welcome constructive feedback because they want to see their shadows as soon as they appear. Feedback is always good—whether "positive" or "negative." Giving and receiving feedback enlivens a community where people are on a similar spiritual path.

The art of giving and receiving feedback occurs most successfully between people who have agreed to make it happen between them. In the new paradigm, this is established at the beginning of the relationship. You can open by saying, "You always have my permission to point out things that I do that do not work for you, or that you believe could be detrimental to myself or others. Do I have the same permission from you?"

I personally like feedback—I welcome it! It is one of the reasons I am where I am today. In our spiritual community, we set up situations for this to happen both formally and informally. A formal setting might be a seminar in which we are learning to increase our social and leadership skills. At any time a participant may stand up and ask for individual feedback on anything from the group. The group may then suggest a change in appearance, speaking mode, attitude, or way of relating. The person receiving these suggestions is not allowed to defend or debate the feedback. In a more informal setting, such as a private conversation, we may spontaneously tell a person how we feel in their presence, trying not to be too harsh or critical. One might say, "Are you aware of the fact that you hang up the phone too abruptly? I feel cut off and cut out." (This last example is feedback I used to hear from others—it had to be pointed out to me. I was not aware of how I made other people feel, and I appreciated knowing. I then had to process why I had developed this habit.)

In an intimate relationship with the person you live with, there is a risk of being less tactful, more critical, and too disapproving. This is because we choose mates who are like the members of our family we are angry with. Unfortunately, we take it out on our mates. How can we give each other feedback that is supportive, tender, and sweet? One agreement you can make is to give feedback on the feedback. "I can hear you when you say it like this, but I cannot hear you when you speak in an angry tone— it scares me and I shut down."

Try asking someone why they are doing something the way they are doing it *before* you criticize their action. Sometimes they have a very good reason which refutes your judgment of them immediately. I wish I could always remember to do this! Let's all try to remember: Be curious, not furious.

Giving Feedback

1. The giver shall first get "permission" to do so, unless you have a prior agreement. Example: "Do you mind if I share with you my feeling about _____?"

2. The giver shall not speak from anger. His heart shall be open as if he were speaking to a very best friend with great respect.

3. The giver shall remember that the issue at hand could also be his own projection. For example, if the giver says, "It feels like you are way too bossy," maybe the other person is *not*, in fact, bossy but the giver imagines this because his own parents were bossy, or he is himself.

4. The giver should say, whenever possible, "What *I* feel is . . . and what *I* would like from you is. . . ." Speaking in terms of how *you* feel or what *you* want is much better than a put down.

Receiving Feedback

1. The receiver shall keep her heart open and not become defensive. If the feedback is accurate, then she shall be very grateful for it. If the feedback is a projection, then it should not bother the receiver anyway.

2. The receiver shall pay attention if she gets this feedback from more than one person. If so, she had better take action quickly.

3. The receiver shall thank the giver instead of defending herself or debating the topic. The receiver may wish to consider adding, "How do you suggest I alter this behavior?"

4. The receiver may take action by asking others to help her with clearing this problem more quickly. Example: "So and so says I hang up the phone too fast and cut people off. I do not want to do that. Please support me by telling me whenever I do that with you."

If couples can see that gentle feedback is a huge benefit, they will advance quite rapidly. If, however, the feedback is too critical, hurtful, or upsetting, it can be destructive in the relationship. People do know and can learn the difference. How do you speak to a friend you adore? How do you speak to someone you totally respect? You have to give and receive feedback in the same way. Probably everyone reading this knows that this is obvious. If you want someone to treat you with respect, you are going to have to learn to treat others that way. It helps to always imagine that your partner is your guru, your teacher, a holy person you are fortunate to be living with.

TRANSMUTING UPSETS

THERE ARE TIMES WHEN ONE OR BOTH PARTNERS FORGET about all the techniques discussed and just "lose it" or "blow it" with each other. When either of you has what I call an "ego attack," which results in a fight, you are *both* left with the task of cleaning it up. How you handle this task is all-important to the future well-being of your relationship. You can either create more separation, or you can become even closer. The outcome is up to you. Train yourself to remember that, "You are never upset for the reason you think," as *A Course in Miracles* would say. If one of you can be quiet and just let the other vent all of his or her feelings, then maybe you can ask, "What is it that is *really* bothering you?" If just one of you can drop the rope, the tug of war will be over. LET IT BE YOU.

No matter what happens, cleaning up afterwards is a major test of your spiritual qualities. Safety is the complete relinquishment of attack; if you don't retract, the person who feels attacked may become so afraid that he or she will just withdraw in the future. Apologies are in order ASAP!

Leonard Orr, the founder of Rebirthing, once said, "The only way to have a perfect relationship is to have two people willing to experience their own perfection." This must be the goal for each partner: A willingness to keep perfecting oneself by self-improvement. Each must remember that this is the purpose of life—and it is a spiritual purpose. So a couple must make self-improvement a top priority. Once this is established and remembered, it becomes much easier to transmute upsets.

Every upset is a "set up." Each person in the upset has to look at his or her part in creating it, *without exception*. When *both* partners take responsibility, healing occurs. This is hardest to do when one person "looks" innocent on the surface, and the other "looks" guilty. In a violent situation, like spousal abuse, you may find it very hard to see how all this applies. In this case, you may need to muster up enough self-love to physically leave the abusive situation. The problem is, of course, that if you do not discover (through self-realization) how you might have attracted, or been attracted to, this kind of situation, it could be recreated in the next relationship.

One of my teachers in India asked me to help a couple in an abusive marriage. I cringed at this assignment because I knew it was going to be very hard. I agreed because I needed to learn more about this, and I liked the two people involved. I was also the one who had "discovered" the abuse. I happened to call after the couple had fought and the wife blurted out the truth to me. I began by rebirthing each of them separately. The man had a basic negative thought, "I AM BAD" (personal lie) from his birth script. This made him do bad things, like hit his wife. The negative reinforcement allowed him to continue to feel bad about himself. The basic negative birth thought of his wife was, "I AM WRONG." Her built-in belief that she was wrong and this demanded punishment. Because of these feelings, she came to believe that she deserved the abuse that followed. Then she would feel that she was wrong to protest it. Years later, after the abuse pattern was cleared, the wife told me that her addiction to smoking was both a punishment and a cover-up for her feelings. She told me that she had given up the addiction to smoking, which was hard. She had given up the addiction to getting herself beaten up, which was even

CREATING
SACRED
RELATIONSHIPS

harder. But the hardest addiction to give up was the thought, "I AM WRONG."

We have to choose not to allow unconscious behavior to continue—and it takes the willingness of *both* parties to clear up an abusive pattern in a relationship. Forgiveness *is* the key to happiness but, in the new paradigm, we would honor *A Course in Miracles'* definition of forgiveness. You do not forgive the old way by implying, "You did this horrible thing, but I am going to be righteous and forgive you anyway." In other words, you do not pardon sins by making them real. You see that there was no sin. You recognize that what the other person did was not real.

A Course in Miracles says, "Every loving thought is true and all else is an appeal for help" (FIP, 1992). This means that even the most offensive action is a twisted way of asking for help. Try to remember this; God asks us to remember this.

Who has shown offending behavior towards you recently? Why not call this person and ask him or her how you can be supportive? Try it! If you love the offending person unconditionally anyway, the conflict is over for you. If correction is in order, offer it from love, not judgment.

We used to ask Babaji at the ashram in India why he had allowed thieves to stay there. He said, "Who else is going to love them?"

MAINTAINING RESPECT

•

IT IS EASY TO RESPECT SOMEONE YOU ARE IMPRESSED with or someone who is doing what you think they should do. But what about when you do not like the other person's behavior—do you lose complete respect for that person? When respect disappears from a committed relationship, the couple often gives up and looks elsewhere.

To keep your partner's respect for you, be willing to see your shadows and be willing to work on them. To maintain respect for your mate when he or she displays his or her shadows, remember this: Shadows are not real. They are like cobwebs covering up the Real Self. The Real Self is God. The Real Self is Love. If you choose to disrespect someone because of their shadows, then you are making their shadows real—you are, in fact, reinforcing them.

Once when a friend came to visit me, I had a spontaneous reaction to what seemed to me his lack of feeling. I started crying. It was an upset, and he felt he should leave because I was so distraught. I could not seem to stop the upset but, as it started to escalate, my companion was able to lie down on the floor near my altar, and I was able to reach over, touch him and say: "I don't care about this. I just want you to know how much I respect you." This cut right through the sewers of our unconsciousness. I wanted him to know I was not losing respect for him. He took my hand and told me how much he respected me. It worked. I felt I had to say it out loud. I did not want him to feel shame, especially since I had not yet become aware of my part in the upset. In the morning, as we were rebirthing in the hot tub, I told him I could see how I was setting him up like one of my family members. I apologized. (Projections happen fast—you have to be on top of them. It takes self-awareness.)

Maintaining respect for someone when they are having a money problem can be very difficult. You might blurt out something horrible like, "You call yourself a man? Why can't you make a decent living?" At times like this it is absolutely crucial to remember that your mate is acting out your father, your mother, or your hidden shadow. You need to find out why this money situation is in your life. If this is a committed relationship, you have to solve the problem together; the first step is to see that you *both* have the problem, even if it is seemingly showing up *over there.*

An example: If a lover refuses to commit and yet I want total commitment, then I have several choices to look at. He could be the part of *me* that is afraid to commit and won't. I could be the part of *him* that really wants to commit. His refusal to commit may be a mirror to show me that my mind is not, in fact, undivided on this subject. I need to respect him for being a mirror.

In some cases, one has to leave a relationship in order to maintain one's own self-respect, but one must always follow up with self-analysis on one's personal agenda.

A COURSE IN MIRACLES
AS A FOUNDATION
FOR THE NEW PARADIGM

IT HAS BEEN SAID THAT *A COURSE IN MIRACLES* IS THE MOST important written work on the planet in two thousand years. The books describe themselves as a required course. We must learn the material sooner or later, but we have free will to decide how long it will take us to learn it. We can wait five months, five years, or five more lifetimes to begin. But why wait? *Sooner or later we have to learn the Course anyway.* What if learning it now gets you out of misery, pain, and death? It can and does. In the rebirthing communities I work with, we try to use it as the underlying foundation of our relationships. To me, it is simply an obvious part of the New Paradigm. I envision couples reading the Course together. I have assigned it to couples who were about to divorce but really did not want to. I have instructed them to read it out loud to each other. This has worked! They have been incredibly happy in their marriages as a result.

Many people tell me that they often have a difficult time reading the Course because of the language. For some, it seems too "Christian" in tone, or too patriarchal (rich in the Father energy). I would like to explain why this is so in hope that you will not avoid reading the books. The reason the Course is Christian in tone is because Christianity is a major influence on the planet. Even if you are not a Christian, you are still greatly influenced by Christian culture, just by living in this society. I could not think or understand with clarity until my false religious notions were corrected. And the Course did that for me. It changed my whole life. So, please don't let the language stop you from reading. If you get stuck on that, try reading my book, *Drinking the Divine*, as a study guide for the Course, or read Marianne Williamson's books and listen to her tapes on the Course.

The whole point of the Course is to show us how we have wasted eons of lifetimes in the wrong state of mind. We have chosen the ego's state of mind instead of the Holy Spirit's state of mind. Until we learn the right state of mind, our relationships will ultimately not work. To have a holy, enlightened relationship, a couple has to know the difference and has to know what to do about the ego. The ego must be turned over to the Holy Spirit to be incorporated properly.

The Course talks about the tyranny of a "special relationship," wherein we regard one individual as more "special" than anyone else, more valuable than ourselves—even more valuable than God! This "special relationship" is the ego's chief weapon to keep us from God.

The Course also discusses how an unholy relationship is based on differences, where each person thinks the other has what he or she has not. They each rob the other and move on. The Course insists that we must learn to have a holy relationship. "A holy relationship starts with a different premise. . . . Each one has looked within and seen no lack. Accepting his completion, he would extend it by joining with another, whole as himself. They come together to share the light."

A Course in Miracles offers the holy relationship as the ideal paradigm for relationships. It also gives you the ideal paradigm for yourself and life. The Course provides clarity in finding out who you really are and what you are really doing here. It is the best gift you can give to yourself and your relationship. The full impact of it can only be appreciated by studying it *directly*. Reading every line is like eating spoonfuls of purified energy. The Course will teach you to see everything differently.

CREATING
SACRED
RELATIONSHIPS

REPLACING THE EGO

SINCE ONE OF THE MAIN PURPOSES OF LIFE IS TO SUBSTI-
tute the ego with the truth, then it is important to be able
to recognize the ego. I have collected various definitions
from my spiritual readings over the years. As far as I can
see, the spiritual masters seem to agree with these definitions, many of which come from *A Course in Miracles* and
the teachings of Meher Baba.

- The ego is a false self you create to replace God.

- The ego is the belief that you are separate from
  God.

- The ego is the belief that you are guilty and
  deserve punishment.

- The ego is fear. It is terrified of love.

- The ego is an illusion.

- The ego is idolatry.

- The ego is a sign of the limited, separated self.

- The ego is a product of ignorance.

- The ego sees the will of God as the enemy and
  denies its existence.

- The ego sees strength as weakness and life as
  death.

- The ego is insane.

- The ego, in competition with God, thinks it is
  victorious.

- The ego stands apart from all, is separate from
  the Infinite.

- The ego dreams of punishment.

- The ego is, quite literally, a fearful thought.

- The ego is represented as a confusion in identification.

- The ego is an affirmation of being separate from the other.

- The ego feeds upon exclusivity.

- The ego nourishes deep distrust.

- The ego expresses itself poignantly through anger and jealousy.

- The ego is made up of desires. Success in obtaining desired objects is success to the ego.

- The ego manifests itself through pride.

- The ego must magnify its attainments in grotesque ways. Self display is very common.

- The ego lives by the idea of "mine."

- The ego makes important that which is unimportant and makes unimportant that which is important.

- The ego subsists upon mundane possessions, such as power, fame, wealth, ability, acquisitions, and accomplishments. However, it always feels empty and incomplete.

- The ego seeks to fortify itself through further acquisitions.

- The ego wants to be superior or inferior.

- The ego may be compared to a driver who has a certain amount of control over the car; but who is in complete darkness about the destination.

- The ego is like an iceberg. The major portions remain submerged.

- The ego says that what opposes God is true.

- The ego is a fenced-off aspect of yourself.

- The ego is separation, limitation, fear, guilt, hate, pain, misery, suffering, disease, depression, and death.

- The ego is your belief in false reality.

Finally, the roots of the ego are in the subconscious mind. The ego is a necessary evil which can be transcended. The whole point of the spiritual path is the slimming down and final release of the ego. This takes time. It usually happens gradually when one is on the path. Divine Love arises in its place. The Course says that the solution is to offer up your ego so that it may be used by the Holy Spirit as a communication device.

DOING SPIRITUAL
PURIFICATION TOGETHER

·

IMAGINE THE FOLLOWING ACTIVITIES AS BEING PART OF your daily life as a couple. Imagine electing one or two to do together every day:

- Rebirthing
- Reading *A Course in Miracles* together
- Chanting
- Writing affirmations
- Fasting
- Being in conscious silence for long periods
- Praying, out loud or in silence
- Fire purification
- Sweat lodges
- Attending seminars
- Listening to spiritual music
- Networking
- Committing to a peace project
- Spending time at an ashram
- Visiting holy places

All of these activities will help you get the most out of life and will help you feel your best.

MUNDUN

Try shaving your heads together! This is called *mundun*. You might have some weird associations with such a practice. But has anyone explained to you its real meaning, especially when done in an ashram? A mundun (headshaving) symbolizes surrendering to God (or a guru). It is a sign of initiation into a spiritual path—a sign of renunciation. Therefore, a mundun takes away old karma and vibrations stored in the hair. It actually uncovers the highest chakras on your head, allowing divine energy to enter your Being. It works psychologically and spiritually by cutting through attachments and mental concepts. It has a rapid healing and rejuvenating effect on the body. It makes one much more creative and strong.

People who do mundun become very clear that their own liberation is more important than anything—even more important than what people might think or say about it or them. Many people who travel to India with me shave their heads. It is totally optional. Mundun is something sacred, and is offered to us for our benefit. Many times, women told me that as they left with me for India, their husbands had said to them, "If you shave your head, don't come back—I will divorce you." I never told these women what to do; usually they would realize that they didn't want to be with a man who was that controlling anyway. For others, when they came home, their husbands got used to it; in the end mundun was the very thing that saved their marriage! By doing mundun, the women would clear that which was destroying their marriage in the first place.

Couples in India often shave their heads together before a wedding ceremony. There must be a reason why this ancient tradition exists even today. Those of us who have experienced it would give this answer: It works. (I have done it three times, once for nine straight months.) Just the other day, a man who went with me to India a year ago told me, "My mundun saved my life!"

A LIFE OF SERVICE

THE REASON HUMAN BEINGS DO NOT HAVE SELF-illumination and continuous joy is because of their *samskaras* or the accumulated imprints of past experience. Samskaras should be entirely removed for total liberation. It is important to understand the law of karma (i.e., you reap what you sow, what you do to another is also done to yourself). Traditionally, great beings removed samskaras by renunciation, solitude, fasting, penance, and by desiring nothing. However, living the life of a complete ascetic seems contradictory to a relationship. The masters say that you can begin to alleviate the conflict by replacing lower values with higher ones. Also, it is recommended that you sublimate your energy into spiritual channels through meditation, devotion, and selfless service.

My master Babaji encourages us to live a life of truth, simplicity, love, service to mankind, and Karma Yoga (work dedicated to God and humanity). He tells us that Karma Yoga is the highest yoga and that it can change our fate. He tells us that idleness is death. Work is worship. Dedicate all of your work to God every day. This will change your life.

The only danger in dedicating your life to serving society (such as charity work) is the possibility of having a false motive for doing so. If you do it for recognition, pride, or for making someone obligated to you, you can do harm to others and yourself by creating more samskaras. Selfless service means that you are willing to give up personal motives. It is also necessary to have spiritual understanding. For example, you might decide to feed the poor. This sounds really wonderful. However, a beggar of food may be creating his own samskaras and you may be inadvertently binding him tighter to his pattern. Cultivating his intellect and raising his self-esteem (so he can get back to work) is a better idea because it is contrary to his pattern. In other words, some service can be a disservice.

Serving a sick person's bodily needs and helping her get back on her feet is a valuable service. Anything that you can do to uplift and advance humanity is good service. Remember, it should always come from the outflowing of your being.

When my husband and I joined the Peace Corps, we were touched more deeply by this experience than anything else in our lives. I consider that time to be the "boot camp" that helped me leap into world service. We were happier then than at any other time in our marriage and we had nothing but ourselves and the purest kind of work—service without pay.

Money is important, but remember the difference between need and desire. You don't always need what you want. Meher Baba once said that *wanting is a source of perpetual restlessness.* If you don't get the thing you want, you are disappointed. If you get it, you want more. Watch out!

I honor Babaji and Meher Baba for inspiring me to write this essay. One thing I have noticed about all the spiritual masters I have studied with was this: They are in bliss. They all serve selflessly and institute projects of incredible value, such as free schools for the poor. Decide which contributions you and your mate will make. Don't be tied to results, but stick to it no matter what.

A COMMUNITY OF MAJESTY

IMAGINE BELONGING TO A GROUP OF FABULOUS PEOPLE who are all working on enlightened ideas together and helping each other to become healed, happy, and whole. I am not talking about belonging to a commune. I am not talking about joining a cult. Quite the opposite. In fact, my book, *Pure Joy*, includes an essay called, "The Difference Between a Cult and a True Spiritual Family." I am talking about a support system.

I envision a paradigm in which you and your mate are part of a supportive group of people who understand what you are doing, and who empower you both to become all that you can be. A community where you can sincerely and openly share the problems you are having in your relationship or with your life and get help with them. It is very important to belong to a spiritual family when you are trying out new paradigms and breaking with cultural tradition. Otherwise you will feel alone, like it is you against the world. A great deal of pressure is taken off your relationship when you have friends you feel intimately close with who nurture you.

Imagine being able to hang out with a group of individuals are totally alive, safe, peaceful, innocent, present, and experiencing their own magnificence. Imagine spending time with future "superbeings" who maintain perfect health and even prevent aging and death! Do you question your qualifications? Well, if you are reading this book, your higher self already knows what is good for you and who you are and what you can be. It is only a question of acting upon this knowledge.

Imagine being with those who experience natural abundance and who want you to experience abundance as well. Imagine people who actually express their Christ-nature! Imagine yourself being able to go to this group and finding a mate if you want one. Imagine being highly productive in such energy. Imagine working with this group on important planetary issues and getting involved in local solutions for the community. Imagine the celebration of having such friends! This is already going on. We have communities of Immortals in many cities of the world already. In fact if you travel to Paris, London, Madrid, Milan, Los Angeles, and many other places, you can check it out. Call the Rebirthing community for information (see page 97).

We lovingly call this family the *Ohana*. This is a Hawaiian word which means "extended family" or "chosen family who breathes together." ("Ha" means "breath" in the Hawaiian language.) This family is dedicated to life itself. I am now introducing the Divine Mother Movement into these communities in order to achieve a higher rebirth.

If rebirthing has not begun in your area, we can bring it to you, right to your doorstep. You gather your friends together and we send a speaker who can train you in the art and science of rebirthing. We can teach you the knowledge of Physical Immortality. We can teach you "Relationships technology" and bring the Relationships Seminars to your community.

To Immortals, their work is their joy. Naturally they want to spiritualize the earth and become warriors against darkness. We invite you to join us. We look forward to knowing you.

NETWORKING AS A
PART OF THE PARADIGM

IN A COMMUNITY OF MAJESTY, EVERYONE IS OPEN TO AND feels good about sharing new knowledge with each other. Networking is natural.

A recent Australian edition of *Elle* magazine had a funny, rather satirical article on networking. It stated that "Networking starts with charm and leads to influence. It is the art of getting what you want while appearing to meet the needs of others." It also described networking as being purely business. The subtext of small talk at parties functions to help you assess whether you want to work for, sleep with, employ, marry, ignore, or manipulate the person you are talking to! Of course, I am not necessarily referring to the use of networking as a trick simply to get things. I *am* talking about a sincere desire to help people make connections with others in a helpful way.

Speaking of parties again, in Sweden they are very up front about socializing and networking together. I went to a party which opened by having everyone in a big circle and each person had to introduce the person next to them, and tell the group what they did that might be interesting.

A Swedish networking party works like this:

1. The host of the gathering stops the party and asks everyone to get into a circle.

2. We interview the person on our right—who they are, what they do, etc.

3. Then we introduce or present that person to the entire group.

This is a wonderful way to readily find out who has the service you might be looking for, and it is all done in a spirit of networking. Everyone is totally willing to support the work of everyone else in that room.

In the paradigm of a community of majesty, people do not withhold good information to be competitive and be "one up" on others. There is no desire for that kind of situation. People want to share with others. They are quick to talk about what works for them (i.e., which body work is really helpful, which healer is really excellent, which technique is the most productive, which seminar is really good, which book is worth reading now).

Unfortunately, the New Age movement has gotten an unfair reputation of being flakey and self-absorbed. But most people in it are concerned with transformation and with sharing their experience of it. That is why they put out networking guides. Their efforts aren't simply for self-promotion.

I look forward to the day when the New Age is accepted as "normal," where people everywhere realize a new awareness of life itself. We envision becoming a vanguard of evolution. We envision people who are willing to become architects of change; who want to transform the planet. Isn't that worth every minute spent networking?

Barbara Marx Hubbard, social evolutionary, talks about a movement of highly evolved beings who join together with other like beings in offering their work, art, and gifts to the world. They become driven to find teammates with whom they can co-create. This, she says, can actually produce "vocational arousal." Imagine that! Imagine your mate's creativity calling forth your creativity and vice versa. That is worth the effort of networking.

Become a good networker! An enlightened being in the New Paradigm is always doing this naturally. Do you doubt that you are a highly evolved being? You are already on the way now to remembering who you are. That is why you need to network with others who will help you remember even more. He or she will offer you information you might not know is available (books, healers, seminars). Return the favor and tell others what you have learned about, heard about, or tried. *A Course in Miracles* says: "Nothing real can be increased except by sharing." (FIP, 1992) The more you share what works, the better it will work for you!

CREATING
SACRED
RELATIONSHIPS

COMMITMENT AND THE
LENGTH OF THE RELATIONSHIP

TWO IMMORTALS ARE COMMITTED TO EACH OTHER forever. This does not mean that they will be together in the same form for their entire lives. Love itself is more important than the form it embodies; relationships are continuously transforming. The relationship never ends, but it might change form. A couple does not say they are "breaking up," but they might say, "the form of our relationship is changing." If immortals want to change the form of their relationships, they try to do it as gracefully as possible, without creating new karmas. You end up more loving as a result of changing the relationship, not more bitter. You want to remain friends with this person. Of course, some couples master how to stay together forever. It's a wonderful goal. Nowadays, there are few convincing reasons for a couple to stay living together for all of life's journey.

In *Seat of the Soul*, author Gary Zukav says that the duration of a spiritual partnership is only as long as appropriate for a couple's evolution. How long is appropriate? He says it is appropriate for them to remain living together as a couple only as long as they grow together. In other words, couples in a new paradigm cannot say for sure that they will stay together forever. Their growth together, he says, may take a whole lifetime, or it may take only six months. Sometimes the Divine brings people together for a short time to grow and to clear karma. In this case, each individual has to have faith that when the other is taken from them, the situation was no longer best for them and God is trying to give them something more appropriate. Immortals learn to trust the universe as perfect. Whatever happens is the perfect thing to happen. The length of their "recovery" from change is dependent on their level of trust in the universe.

A relationship should always make you stronger, not weaker. I am careful not to tell people what to do should they ask me if they should stay together. What I do say is this: "Pray for this relationship to heal for something better for both of you (that way, either outcome is a win). I might ask this: "If you had no fear, no guilt, and were not worried about what others would say, what would you do?" They often say, "I would leave." Then they must face the fact that staying might not be ethical. I would also tell them to pray for Divine Right Action.

Most people seem to want a long-lasting, immortal, monogamous relationship that will go on forever. It is a beautiful vision and one we support. If making a commitment helps you free yourself from your ego, then a commitment makes you free. Period. Think about THAT! Marriage is a hindrance or an advantage depending on how it is handled. In the new paradigm, couples may not want to get married, but as Zukav says, if they do choose to get married, they will know that they need to infuse the marriage with this new archetype. In any relationship, married or not, success depends upon consciousness.

CREATING
SACRED
RELATIONSHIPS

TWO APPROACHES

•

ONE APPROACH IS THE "STAYING TOGETHER NO MATTER what" approach. This involves the "till death do us part" attitude in the old paradigm.

Then there is the second approach, called "serial monogamy," which is a growing trend. With this approach, a person commits exclusively to a partner for a significant period of time, but moves on if and when the relationship stops growing. They go on to commit exclusively to another partner for another unspecified period of time, and so on. People who can handle this approach do not feel guilt about having short relationships. Many people feel it is illogical to think that one partner is going to suit them for many decades. They may even say at the beginning of a relationship that they are not prepared to promise that they will feel the same way in ten years time.

This may be hard for many of us to accept. However, those of us seeking new paradigms will say that it is a lot more honest than having multiple affairs. Serial monogamy is not suited for everyone, however. Psychotherapist Diana Laschelles states that this relationship pattern only suits people with a lot of confidence who are socially very comfortable, who can separate easily, recover fast, and move on. Some admit that there is a danger of becoming jaded. Others complain that this system cannot work with children in the picture. Still others think it can; they say it is not good to teach children to stick together in "martyred misery." This whole idea has even been called "the 90s way of loving" (Laschelles, January 1994).

It remains to be seen whether people will find ongoing satisfaction with this lifestyle, but it needs to be discussed, as it is becoming more and more common. What I find most interesting about articles and discussions on this subject is that people usually say in the end that if they could have a relationship that was truly alive and stayed truly alive, they would not mind staying it in forever. They don't seem to want serial monogamy just for its own sake or just for variety. What people seem to be searching for is something that does not die.

You can use the serial monogamy approach or you can try to stay in the same relationship forever. The choice is yours. Either way, one has to learn how to keep these relationships alive. Keeping your relationship alive requires enlightenment.

Achieving enlightenment also has two approaches. The traditional way is to simply let life itself process you. By going through the "school of hard knocks", and by experiencing life after life of numerous incarnations, the soul is finally forced to learn enlightenment. It wakes up completely and becomes whole. The problem with this method is that it is very slow, especially if one is not conscious that enlightenment is the goal.

The second approach makes a conscious choice to commit to self-analysis and spiritual purification on a regular, daily basis—dissolve and be reborn again each day. To me, this is easier, quicker, more wonderful and *the point of this book.*

SEX IN THE NEW PARADIGM

A COURSE IN MIRACLES WOULD SAY THAT ALL THAT matters about sex is whether you are in the ego's thought system with it or are you in the Holy Spirit's thought system with it. If you are in the Holy Spirit's thought system, then it will be a sacred, holy experience.

As Osho (Rajneesh) once said: "The primal energy of sex has the reflection of God in it. Sex *is* Divine. It is the energy that creates new life. Therefore you should accept sex with joy and acknowledge its sacredness. When a man approaches his wife, he should have a sacred feeling, as if he were going to a temple. As a wife goes to her husband, she should be full of the reverence one has nearing God. Orgasm is for the momentary realization of samadhi. The ego vanishes. Orgasm is a state of self effacement. *This* is the reason we are really so attracted to it. It is wrong to fill man with antagonism toward sex."

In tantric teachings sexual love represents sacrament, its ultimate goal is union with God. There are even books on how you and your mate can use Tantric sex to achieve physical immortality together (Zitko, 1985).

Immortals can tell you the difference between the "old sex" and the "new sex." They experienced old sex before they understood the concept of physical immortality and worked out their death urge. They had old sex before they learned to rebirth themselves and knew how to use the breath to prolong orgasm. Old sex was before the subconscious was clear of the fear of letting go. New sex is part of their new life as immortals. They feel safe enough to handle a lot more energy in the body without the unconscious fear of death. They feel safe enough to let go. Immortals know how to use sex for rejuvenation.

The space a couple chooses for lovemaking should be like a temple. I recommend an altar in the room. I recommend soft music or chanting. I recommend making the whole space as lovely as possible. There should always be fresh flowers, candles, beautiful objects around, and soothing, sensual fabrics. Televisions, library books, stacks of stuff, and old bedding is not conducive to holiness. Doing a simple puja, or worship, at the altar beforehand will put you in the right frame of mind, even something as simple as waving incense before pictures of the holy ones. Turn the experience over to God.

Think very carefully about your lover. Some teachers will tell you that there can be karmic *exchange* through sexual activity. Sex is not a simple matter of connect-disconnect. Some say that the linking that results from one single sexual activity may last for approximately fourteen months on higher planes. That means that the karmic link does not dissolve until fourteen months later. So, think about the consequences *before* you sleep with someone tonight who may have slept with someone else last night. Sleeping with multiple partners *can* have karmic as well as bodily consequences. It is important to think about "safe sex" on both a physical and a spiritual level.

CHILDREN IN THE NEW PARADIGM

ENLIGHTENED COUPLES KNOW THAT CHILDREN ARE OLD souls in little bodies, and they treat them with that respect. They know that the children who have been born in recent years could, in fact, be of a higher energy vibration than their parents.

Seeing your own child as your "guru" may be a shocking concept at first, but consider this: Children are three-dimensional projections of your subconscious mind. Children act out your subconscious mind and reflect it back to you. This may drive you nuts, but if you understand this dynamic, it will improve your relationship with your children to no end. Instead of punishing them, consider the alternative of asking yourself what your child is trying to reflect back to you when there is a problem. What you suppress, your children will express. Your child *is* your guru. The principle in metaphysics is this: Love takes upon itself your negatives so you can see them more clearly. Your child, out of love, may "take on" what you are suppressing and show it to you, for your own healing. Listen to your children.

You may already know the work of John Bradshaw on the subject of families. He suggests that the best way to be a parent is to heal our own wounds from our own childhood. Your own children will give you an opportunity to do that. As your child goes through his or her developmental stages, your own wounded issues will come up at each stage.

Enlightened couples want to have what we call a "conscious conception," a "conscious pregnancy," and a "conscious delivery." Each is designed to reduce birth trauma. (See my earlier book, *Ideal Birth*.) Enlightened couples also understand that a child is not a blank slate at birth (read *Other Lives, Other Selves* by Dr. Roger Woolger).

When a new child comes in, it can be a crisis. There is a danger that the couple disconnects too much; that one parent will transfer idyllic attachment to the child and form a "new" couple—with the child! The other mate gets pushed out. Or the couple could go to the other extreme and leave the child out! Enlightened couples try to find a balance.

It thrills to me to see young children rebirthing very early. Imagine having your birth trauma cleared out before becoming an adult! In Madrid, I simply loved to see Sua, age five, go under water with her own snorkel, and do her own wet rebirthing. Sua's parents are rebirthers; her psychic and intuitive abilities are highly developed as no one has ever censored them.

Teach your child that thoughts create results.

SELF-ACCEPTANCE, SATISFACTION, AND PEACE OF MIND

IN THE OLD PARADIGM, WE MEASURE OUR SUCCESS AND satisfaction by what we accomplish and possess. Social status or success in business or career have too often been indications of success as a person. If our self-worth depends on something outside of ourselves, such as a high salary, costly possessions, or "good" kids, then we feel worthless inside if those things are not up to par with those of others.

The goal in the new paradigm is to always feel complete self-acceptance, satisfaction, and peace of mind, no matter what is going on around you. If you think this is easy, think again. The ego will tempt you to think that you need the money, recognition, possessions, partner, kids, etc., in order to feel valuable as a person. The ego will set you up to feel frustrated one way or another. Your personal life might be perfect, but then your career suffers . . . or vice versa.

The ego actually encourages frustration, deprivation, desperation, aggravation, limitation, and humiliation. You may think you feel those feelings because of what is not working in your life, but what is not working in your life is, in fact, a result of those feelings. Even if you took all the externals away and went into a cave for a long time, you would feel dissatisfaction and a lack of peace of mind anyway. The ego must be cleared. The point is this: As long as your ego dominates your life, as it does for most people, you will set up situations to act out your frustration and lack of peace of mind. You will unconsciously set up your relationship or business not to work so you can go back to that feeling of frustration.

The ego *is* an addiction. The ego says, "Seek love and never find it" and, "If you find it, get rid of it." It wants you always to be in the frustration of the search. It does not want satisfaction. One of the most complicated aspects of the ego in relationships is called the "incest pattern." In this pattern, you are attracted to someone you cannot have, and you are no longer attracted to the one you have. This also results in "unrequited love" which seems more passionate.

In the New Paradigm, the couple sees these traps. They understand how the incest pattern operates and how the ego operates. In the New Paradigm, the couple understands how easy it is to sabotage love and satisfaction. They know how to stop their tendencies to "kill off" the relationship. They are each more comfortable with peace instead of drama.

Final detachment and enlightenment means that each feels satisfaction, self-acceptance, and peace of mind whether they are in a relationship or are alone. Either way is okay!

MONEY

IT IS DANGEROUS TO BECOME SO FIXATED ON OUR personal wealth and the pursuit of material possessions and prestige that we lose concern about the welfare of others. There is also a danger of going to the opposite extreme and having a money rejection complex. Balance is in order. The only point I want to emphasize here is the importance of an enlightened couple getting clear on their relationship to money and spirituality. This, I feel, is best described in the *The Abundance Book* by John Price. He explains that, "God does not provide us with money and homes . . . [God] gives us *divine substance*." This substance is available to all. This substance is like creative energy which flows through the mind of man and externalizes itself as money, homes, or whatever. This substance is molded by our thoughts and therefore externalizes itself as a mirror of our thoughts.

It makes no sense for enlightened beings to have poverty consciousness. Poverty is of the ego, *A Course in Miracles* reminds us. Only *you* can deprive yourself of anything.

It is important to consider the spiritual principle of detachment. The renunciation of external things is not as important as letting go of internal cravings. This detachment disengages the soul from entanglement. One of the chief forms by which the frustrated ego expresses itself is greed. Greed is a state of restless craving for power and possessions. But when these desires are fulfilled, you find you are still unsatisfied. This increases feelings of greed. You can get stuck in unhappiness by wanting more. Yogananda advises us to banish the imaginary hope that happiness will come from worldly fulfillments. A worldly person can become so invested in his material cravings that he will lose interest in other things if they don't have a direct bearing on his cravings.

Consider the fact that you can have glorious satisfaction by moving toward a life of service. What is the purpose of money anyway? Money is a tool for healing the world. After you create it, use money for what it does best.

If you are doing what you love and manifesting the Divine Plan of your life, the money will follow. By the way, here is one test to take to see if you are in the right career:

1. Would you continue your work if you were not getting paid for it?

2. Would you continue what you are doing if you had only one year to live? Be totally honest.

In the New Paradigm of the enlightened couple, each is doing something they *want* to do. Each is clear about the Divine Plan for his or her life. If you still have doubts as you ready yourself for the New Paradigm, try this affirmation: "I am now willing for the Divine Plan of my life to manifest."

THE NEED FOR SPACE

JUDITH SILLS, PH.D., WROTE THE FOLLOWING PERCEPTIVE observation: "A good marriage accommodates deeply contradictory needs: Sometimes you feel very close and sometimes you need to pull apart. There are rhythms." If marriage, or any committed relationship, means total attachment, periods apart will be scary. On the other hand, if one craves independence, then intense intimacy will become overwhelming. To have balance, you must become comfortable with both states. In the New Paradigm, a strong couple can go back and forth easily between attachment and independence.

Sometimes when one mate in an enlightened couple is in a heavy process, it is a good idea for that person to be alone. If you are both stuck at the same time and cannot get through it, then a little distance is definitely a good idea to consider. You can work out a lot in silence. Visit an ashram or enroll in a workshop. Do not rule out leaving town if you must. In a new paradigm you do not want to interfere with your partner's love for him or herself. I am not saying that it is always easy. Sometimes you want your mate to stay with you and he or she wants to do something else. You have to let go and it has to be okay. You don't own your partner. After a while, you will see how healthy it is to have periods of time apart from each other.

I was tested on this principle recently in my own relationship. My new companion was with me in Spain and we were having a marvelous time. I thought he was going to stay with me continuously until I left to travel to other parts of Europe. One day, he suddenly decided he had to leave for Barcelona to do some work, and then return to his home in another country. It was a spontaneous decision and it caught me by surprise, especially since we weren't having any problems. The opposite was true. I could not figure out why he had to leave the next day. It did not make sense. Why couldn't he stay two more days? I expressed my disappointment. I felt like complaining a little. His comment shocked me. He said, "Now you are acting rather like an ordinary person. We, as immortals, have hundreds of years we can be together." I was so stunned I could not speak. After some serious thought I realized he was right and told him so. He told me I was wonderful. I think his intimacy quotient was filled though maybe he did not realize it. He simply wanted SPACE—he wanted to go and he went. The next time we met in Santa Fe, he tested me again. He left one day earlier than expected this time. I wanted him to stay and I knew that he could. But instead of whining, I lay on the couch and relaxed with the cat. As he was going out the door, I said, "It took me twelve trips to India to be okay with this moment . . . I am shocked that I am not upset." The funny thing was that in both cases, his leaving turned out to be the perfect thing to happen. I needed to be tested on those days.

Women and men have different styles of processing. You need to consider your mate's methods; do not always expect them to be like yours. In the New Paradigm, this is very important to understand ahead of time and to discuss. Women like to talk, sometimes men don't, but this is changing.

THE FEAR OF CHANGE

WE MUST NOW RE-EXAMINE THE IDEA OF CHANGE AND what it really means. We are not talking about changing the Real Self. It needs no change. What needs to change is the *idea* of who you are—the ego's idea of limitation. If you look at it in those terms, why wouldn't you want to change? If your mate, or anyone else, wants you to change, what they want changed are the parts that are illusions— the traits that hurt you or others. People who are threatened by someone who insists that they change do not understand this point.

Some people don't ever want their intimate relationship to change. Some couples think they should stay like the couple they were when they first met. They will never get to experience what they *could become* together!

Many articles on relationships imply that a man can change only if a crisis in his life triggers it. And furthermore, whatever does influence a man to change, it better not be his lover! Warning after warning is given that if a man is under pressure to change at home, he will feel more secure with a mistress who likes him the way he is. Some advise that if you want to keep a man, never ever criticize him. I have been reading this for decades. There is actually some truth to it, *if* men are operating in the old paradigm.

I certainly do not recommend criticism. What I *do* suggest is opening yourself to a New Paradigm where conscious willingness to advance is one of the main components. This means you have to change—especially your limitations and your ego-based negative thoughts. An enlightened couple desires and welcomes change. They welcome feedback. They know, with certainty, that we have all been asleep spiritually; that we need to wake up. The word for couples to focus on would be ENCOURAGEMENT. Each encourages the other to advance.

Spiritual advancement begins when there is a radical change in the outlook of a worldly person. The pursuit of the desires connected to the body is not longer a motivating factor. To the spiritually advanced person, the values of the soul predominate. Then the body is used as an instrument to help achieve this advancement.

When you attempt to jump to a new level of consciousness, the ego puts up a battle. Fear has to be confronted. You need effective tools to deal with fear. In rebirthing, we inhale love and exhale fear. We say, "Fear Forward!" Fears are due to thoughts—thoughts that can be *changed*. If you are resistant to changing old habits and addictions, then your need to clear, or "process," the fear of letting go of these things. Rebirthers are trained to help you with this struggle.

Sometimes, people are afraid of change because of their first change—going from the liquid darkness of the womb to the harshly lit atmosphere of the delivery room. This memory remains somewhere within them. Rebirthing can work out the trauma of birth.

MINI SUPPORT GROUPS

THE COMMUNITY OF MAJESTY CAN BE USED AS A SOURCE from which to draw and create your own mini support groups. Those people you gravitate towards in the community can be brought together, not only to hang out and have fun with, but also to support your process and to assist you and your mate with problems you might have. Immortals like doing this for each other. They want everyone around them to feel as good as they do, and be as alive as they are. They want more people to play with and work with; my experience is that they are very good at helping new people to feel comfortable. A new member just has to have enough self-esteem to ask for support. A member in the community might ask: "Will you process me on this problem in my relationship?" The other person will probably answer with one of the following responses:

1. "I would be glad to. Do you want to do it on the phone, over here, over there, in a restaurant, or in a sauna?"

2. "This sounds like it will take a long time, but I don't have time today. Maybe X can help you now, or maybe I can see you tomorrow."

3. "I am willing to do it if you will also process me. Let's do a trade."

4. "I think you need a rebirthing instead. Call so and so."

5. A professional with a lot of training might say this: "I charge this much for that kind of consultation. If you don't have the money, you could pay me later."

If you are new to the community, call up an old timer and ask him or her who is the right person to call about a problem.

Old timers in a mini support group are not afraid to be processed by someone, even in front of everyone else in the group. Nothing is hidden. Everyone considers processing as being for the purpose of healing. Sometimes as many as three people are needed to process someone. The team process is faster and more intense. Begin with one person and build up to it.

When Immortals get together they sometimes deliberately make up new processes—almost like a parlor game, except that there is always a sacred aspect to it. If someone does not like it, they have enough self-esteem to say they do not want to do it. Everyone can do what they please. For example, when someone obviously needs to share and get support, but has a hard time asking for support, team players usually know this. They might even prompt: "Is there anything that you would fear sharing with me because it is too difficult, embarrassing, inappropriate, trivial, or whatever? Why not share it with me now?" Usually the person withholding is secretly relieved and opens up. If not, the support team might say, "Are you willing to look at, and tell us about your fear of sharing?" and so on, until the fear is finally expressed and cleared in as safe an environment as possible.

"A BREEZEFUL OF PEACE"

A great being will go to any extent to become devoid of anger. I have written about the dangers and consequences of anger in almost every one of my books. The best treatise for avoiding anger and fighting is in *Loving Relationships Book II.*

Remember this: *A Course in Miracles* states that anger is never justified. Meher Baba says that anger "feeds the limited ego and is used for domination and aggression." (Meher Baba, 1987). Anger and fighting are not part of the New Paradigm. Enlightened couples want peace and resolution. That does not mean they don't have problems. But they know how to find solutions. They can ever disagree without an upset.

A Course in Miracles says that the first obstacle to peace is the desire to get rid of it. We are so addicted to anger and conflict that we use anger as an excuse to get rid of peace, which feels unfamiliar. Anger feeds on itself.

It is our moral and spiritual responsibility as enlightened beings to learn to live without anger. Remember: Attack causes separation. Communication ends separation.

Some clients actually try to convince me that they cannot control their anger. I ask them, "Who is in control of your anger?" This stops them in their tracks a bit. Then they try to say, "I am addicted to it—I cannot get out of my addiction." I tell them that an addiction is just a stubborn refusal to get off of something. I try to get them to face the cause of their anger. I also try to get them to face their fear of giving up the use of it as a controlling device. Then and only then will I start their rebirthing.

My teacher, Babaji, was the most articulate I have ever heard anyone be on this subject. He taught that anger should not be suppressed (that it is bad for the body) nor does it have to be expressed (that it hurts others). What you do is change the thought causing the anger. In the New Paradigm, we confess the thought (instead of dumping). Then we breathe out the heavy energy; either in a rebirthing, or if that is not possible, by engaging in any strenuous, physical activity until it leaves us.

While I was talking to a photographer here in Australia who did a photo shoot for me, he told me an amazing story. He and his wife had been having a "blue" for a whole week awhile back. A "blue," in Australia, means fighting a lot. She had to get away so she went to their old friends who offered her a lot of drugs and booze. She got no help at all. Then she decided to come and stay at the "urban ashram" of the Gold Coast. She stayed here a few days and began her first private rebirthings. When she came home she was a changed person. She told him rebirthing was better than any drug. He told me he could not get over how nothing bothered her now. She was just like a breezeful of peace. He has also started rebirthing and loves it.

CREATING
SACRED
RELATIONSHIPS

INTIMACY WITH EVERYONE

NOTICE HOW YOU JUST FELT WHEN YOU READ "INTIMACY with Everyone." Most people react by exclaiming, "Oh, my God, is she recommending sex with everyone?" No, I am not. I am recommending intimacy—emotional and spiritual intimacy.

A Course in Miracles teaches us that if you love only parts of reality, you do not know what love means. If you love unlike God, who knows no special love, how can you understand it? As Children of God, all human beings together comprise the Sonship. By desiring a special relationship with only one other human being, we limit our love to only one small segment of the Sonship. Somewhere inside us we intuitively know we have forsaken the totality of the Sonship. This knowledge creates guilt in our minds and our relationships. Guilt houses fear; love where fear has entered is not perfect.

God is not partial, so why are we? If we develop our consciousness to the level required, we can be in love with everyone. That is what the spiritual master does. He falls in love with everyone. In an enlightened relationship, loving everyone is not a threat to either partner because each understands that the Holy Spirit is in everyone. In a Community of Majesty, intimacy with everyone occurs naturally. Jealousy and sibling rivalry are addressed and dealt with openly.

Most people, even enlightened beings who are in a committed relationship, prefer monogamy. Having an outside sexual relationship would dilute the significance of their relationship and be a distraction. It is logical that if a person wants to have an open relationship, he or she should find someone else who also wants, or can tolerate, that model. Different cultures vary somewhat as regards monogamy. In Europe, it seems to be more acceptable to have open affairs. Secret affairs usually don't turn out well anywhere in the world simply because their conception is without integrity (being hidden) and the subsequent sub-conscious guilt creates havoc, pain, and more bad karma. Some people think they want to have several open sexual relationships at once. But they often find such a situation too complicated to be practical.

Affairs often start because a couple's intimate life becomes neglected. It has often been said that women crave intimacy and men avoid it. Perhaps you have heard about men who are described by women as "emotionally crippled" and who even defend their emotional unavail-ability as "normal"! A woman who is used to intimacy might try to force it upon a man. Psychologist Helen Formaini believes that men actually see danger in affilia-tion and safety in isolation. They fear women as they fear self-knowledge. This will change as we all get into the male-female balance in the New Paradigm.

What if everyone (men and women) has some fear of intimacy? If we deny ourselves this opportunity for self-knowledge, how can we fully develop our capacity for love and tenderness? Fear of intimacy is not only a personal shortcoming, it is very bad for our health and can lead to tragic consequences. We need to stop protecting ourselves from hurt and develop the emotional courage to take the risk of staying open.

THE HEALED BODY

IN THE OLD PARADIGM, PEOPLE EXPECT TO GROW OLD, get sick, and then die—and so they do. To Immortals, the healed body is a reality, not a fantasy. An ageless body is a reality, not an illusion. But first a couple has to be willing to reach truth through purification and the release of ego identification.

Each partner of an enlightened couple knows that the mind rules the body; that the body is at the mercy of the mind. Each understands that their thoughts alone can cause them pain. Each also knows how to clear their thoughts to get out of, and prevent pain, sickness, and death. Each understands that no one affects them but themselves. They understand that all illness is mental illness and that the physician is their own mind. Pain and symptoms are self-deceptions that can disappear when seen for what they are.

An enlightened couple understands that each must assist the other in healing the mind in order to heal the body. They understand that all healing is release from the past and from fear. They do not collude with another's false reality of sickness. By using the body correctly as a communications device, instead of using it for attack, they are already on the right track towards maintaining a healthy body. They have accepted the truth of who they are, thereby ending the separation each had created. They also know that the guiltless mind cannot make a body that suffers. So innocence sets them free.

An enlightened couple is devoted to the well being of the other. Neither hesitates to process the other when symptoms arise. If they are in a Community of Majesty, the other members gladly assist in this process also. If one person in the relationship feels he cannot quickly and properly process his mate back to a healthy reality, a rebirther is recommended. If the rebirther feels the case is too tricky, she will not hesitate to call in others. In some cases, up to three rebirthers help restore a person to health. Rebirthers have great confidence in the power of rebirthing to heal. They know that individuals heal themselves with their own minds and they are highly trained to facilitate this phenomenon rapidly with this breathing miracle.

There is no shame in calling in a Western doctor also. It is often necessary if a mind has too much fear of self-healing or is still addicted to the Western medical model. However, alternative forms of healing are recommended first.

In the Community of Majesty, many great healers, such as acupuncturists, body harmonists, reflexologists, rolfers, and chiropractors are easily available.

SHIFTING FROM THE OLD PARADIGM TO A NEW ONE

·

I DO NOT PRETEND THAT ONE SHOULD EASILY JUMP INTO this paradigm. It is a gradual process. But I am a visionary and I do feel we need a vision. I myself am trying to learn how to make this shift smoothly. Sometimes even I miss the mark.

Perhaps the first step is to realize how *stuck* we all are in the old models. Would you rather be in a role or would you rather be your real self? This is what you have to decide. Just because a model has shaped our perceptions for thousands of years does not mean it is right, nor does it mean it cannot be changed.

Today a friend came over and told me about all of her marriage problems. She complained that her husband would do things like make her pick up every little thing she left around immediately, but then he would leave his tools around and never pick them up himself. He would not listen to criticism but he endlessly criticized her. He never listened to her feelings. And all he talked about was business. She resented that he was not as deeply involved in the enlightenment movement as she was. He was still hanging onto the old paradigm and she felt she was ready to switch to a new one.

To help my friend face the conflict she was experiencing with her husband, I gave her John Gray's book, *Men Are from Mars, Women Are from Venus*. His extensive research on how to deal with the differences between men and women, especially in communication, makes this excellent reading for couples in transition. It makes the old paradigm more tolerable and workable. I still find the old paradigm exhausting and I was exhausted after reading the book, despite all the good points in it. I no longer want to wrestle with it. However, it is true that, as a rule, men excel in qualities of the head and women in qualities of the heart. We do need ways to bridge the gap until everyone is in male-female balance inwardly.

My friend came back after reading the book and said, "This is all well and good and I can learn to accommodate those differences that are very male, but what if he won't accommodate the differences which are female?" Her husband would not read the book. So there you are. I asked her if she had discussed their priorities in life with him. She told me yes, but his priorities were financial. Hers were spiritual. I wondered if they would get through this. A few days later she told him she had to return the book to me and suddenly he decided to read it! He actually admitted to her that he had been wrong.

At some point on our spiritual path, we have to overcome sexual duality, cultural programming, and assumed roles. Perhaps step one is to see just how stuck we are in our gender identification. If you are over-identified with your particular gender, you are fragmented and you will think you need the opposite sex to feel whole. This must be resolved from within, not without. All we really have to do is to process our ego. The problematic ego is the same for both sexes. Read *A Course in Miracles* and decide for yourself if this is true.

A NEW PARADIGM FOR SINGLES

IF YOU ARE SINGLE AND NOT IN AN INTIMATE RELATION-
ship, you are probably either enjoying your freedom, or
longing for a mate. For a woman, craving a man is often
the ego's version of wanting to find God. For a man,
yearning for money is often the ego's version of wanting
to find God. In other words, these are substitutes for
God—the ego tricks you into thinking that finding the
right mate or having money will satisfy you.

The longing to go back to the Source is present in
each of us from the very time we think we have separated
from it. But we are unconscious of what that real longing
is until we enter upon a true spiritual path. Why not take
advantage of all the time you have for yourself as a single
person that would otherwise be spent working on a relationship? Use that time in the wisest way possible and
commit to a spiritual path. You will find your loneliness
disappearing.

If you are single, *accept* that you have chosen solitude
and realize that it was not forced upon you by bad luck,
fate, lack of potential mates, or something being wrong
with you. You are not a victim, *ever*. For some reason, your
higher self has chosen to be alone for this period. Perhaps
there is something you want to learn from this experience.
Perhaps you fear being in a relationship. Whatever your
reasons, you can "create a mate" whenever you are ready.
You can process the fear of involvement, whenever you are
ready.

Even if you do not want to be in a relationship, it is
still a wonderful idea to be in the Community of Majesty
for your emotional fulfillment and for your spirituality.

The friendships and support given to you will bring you much happiness. Or, if you are actively looking for a mate, is there a better place to find one than in a spiritual community?

Facing life alone, without a community or a teacher, is too difficult a choice for many of us. You cannot understand yourself alone. *A Course in Miracles* says, "Alone we can do nothing, but together our minds fuse into something whose power is far beyond the power of our separate parts" (FIP, 1992). Our function is to work *together*.

There are so many communities you can join which contribute to making a difference in the world. All you have to do is pick up the phone and offer yourself. If you want a rebirthing-immortality community to join, you can make it happen. All you do is pick up the phone and call this number: (800) 690-5739 in the USA and ask about the local groups or how you can get one started where you are.

CELIBACY

IF YOU ARE CELIBATE, REMEMBER THAT YOU HAVE CHOSEN to be so and that you are not a victim. It might be an unconscious choice or it might be a conscious one, but it is still your choice.

Many single people I know would agree with George Leonard, who said: "Casual, recreational sex is hardly a feast. . . . It is a diet of fast food served on plastic containers!" Most people on a spiritual path are no longer interested in superficial experiences or in being sidetracked. Read "The Problem with Sex" by Meher Baba in *Discourses*. He writes about the issues of repression and indulgence. Repression of sex does not ultimately work because you then end up becoming obsessed with it. But if you go out and try indulging your sexual appetite, you will feel a bondage of the senses from which you will long for release. The only way out is to realize that both of these extremes will vanish once you overcome craving.

Being on a spiritual path helps tremendously. Those who are fortunate enough to be awakened by a Perfect Master, such as Meher Baba or Babaji, develop enough wisdom to free them from the traps of repression and indulgence. What Meher Baba recommended, when he wrote *Discourses*, was to choose celibacy or marriage and not to accept a cheap compromise between the two. In the New Paradigm, a committed relationship is in the "category" of a marriage. Nowadays, not everyone wants to be married. But I do believe that promiscuity is not a healthy alternative. The main point here is that for celibate individuals and married individuals, the path of inner life is the same (Meher Baba, 1987).

What do we mean by "sexual" anyway? If it simply means having intercourse during which "something is done"—an exercise of power and the achievement of a goal occurs—then many spiritual people find it not worth much anyway. Sex should never be about getting a job done! Most spiritual people prefer waiting until they can create sex that is holy and miraculous. In the meantime, conscious celibacy can lead to high states of abundant creativity.

It might be ideal for you, at this time, to open yourself to the possibility of having one of the most significant relationships you can possibly have in a lifetime: A relationship with a Perfect Master. Open yourself to the pure and divine love which can consume all your weaknesses. Serving a Master is the quickest way of realizing him. Allegiance to a Master is allegiance to your higher Self. When my gurus, Babaji, Muniraj, or Shastriji, gave me a treatment, an assignment, or a *lila* (divine play to unravel your mind), I never questioned or argued. I always looked at myself instead. This has helped me a great deal in relationships. I see any mate as my guru and try to see any upset as an opportunity to look at myself. Try it. Use any upset as an opportunity to look at yourself. Thank your partner for this opportunity.

During my periods of aloneness and celibacy, I remained fulfilled and happy. Helping Babaji to spread the truth to a suffering humanity has always been and continues to be more satisfying than anything else.

MARRIAGE

WHEN I ASK MY SINGLE FRIENDS HOW THEY FEEL ABOUT marriage, they usually say, "Why should I get married when nearly all of my married friends are unhappy in marriage or getting divorced?" Marriage is an intensification of most human problems. Therefore, it cannot be based on limited motives, such as sex or financial gain since it could rapidly deteriorate into selfishness. Behind the words of my friends, I hear a secret wish for some other way they could again have the dream of marriage— the secure refuge and safe haven they imagined. They wish for a new partnership which could actually work.

I really appreciate Gary Zukav's thoughtful work on new paradigms. In *Seat of the Soul*, he points out how easy it is for souls who marry to fall into the orbit of the old, no longer functional archetype of marriage. He states that souls have to create a new archetype and reinterpret marriage. For example, make it a sacred commitment to assist each other's spiritual growth as I've mentioned earlier. Partners are together for the evolution of their souls; they *recognize* their equality. They move toward what he calls "authentic empowerment," as opposed to the old archetype which reflects power as external. An authentically powerful person is humble and harmless, treasures life, forgives, takes responsibility, and sees perfection in everything. *Seat of the Soul* will wisely deprogram and reprogram you.

One of my friends recently got divorced, but continues to live with her husband. They are much happier now. She claims that they had to get divorced to break free from their marriage roles. She is as monogamous as ever, so it has nothing to do with sex. She and her husband are simply reinventing their relationship. Their marriage has been recycled, so to speak! In the old model, which they adhered to for many years, her husband avoided all self-examination and was a typical, macho male. She left him for six months. He re-evaluated his life, took seminars, and changed totally—and he *likes* it. She came back. If you are married and would like your relationship to change, you don't necessarily have to separate or get divorced to force that change, but you may need to invest a lot more of yourself in a spiritual process which will help you discover this path of real transformation.

Meher Baba said, "Marriage has to be undertaken [by both parties] as a real spiritual adventure for exploring the higher possibilities of the Spirit" (Meher Baba, 1987). From that space, you, as two enlightened souls, can offer your united love and service to humanity. This takes conscious and deliberate cooperation and it is the model I recommend.

There still seems to be a universal desire for marriage, maybe it still exists because of the cosmic power of love to draw everything back to oneness. This oneness we are looking for is a oneness with God—this should be our goal, whether we are married or single.

My conclusion is this: What you do with marriage determines whether you achieve bondage or liberation. Obviously, our goal is to become liberated within the structure that marriage offers. So, ask yourself: Are you in the Ego's thought system with your marriage or the Holy Spirit's thought system? If you feel yourself trapped by the Ego, then it may be time to consider a new model or paradigm for your relationship.

WHAT IS THE FUTURE
OF THE FAMILY?

THE ECONOMIC RATIONALE FOR MARRIAGE IS DISAPPEAR-
ing. For a growing number of women, remaining single is
a very satisfying choice. Studies indicate that women initi-
ate roughly 60 percent of divorces in the United States.
During the 80s, articles appeared stating that there was
actually a man shortage in America and some women pan-
icked. But then Susan Faludi wrote a book called *Backlash*
in which she stated, "To justify their positions of power,
men promote studies and statistics purporting to show
the dire consequences of women's growing independence,
even if the statistics are WRONG!" (Faludi, 1992). Since
then articles have begun to appear claiming that there is
no shortage of men after all. *New Woman* magazine
observed that, "Many movies are designed to convince
women that they would be happier and healthier if they
married, had children, and stayed home. But only 38 percent of women believe the ideal family is where men work
and women stay at home. Women do not want to be full-
time homemakers" (January 1994).

The debate between the sexes continues today. Some
women feel that men blame the Women's Movement for
the decline of the traditional family. They feel it has been
implied that their career aspirations are selfish. Economic
necessity as much as professional satisfaction compel
women to work and so they resent these claims. They
blame men for leading the rebellion against family values.
Movies which extol the virtues of men who can stay single the longest are but one example of this rebellion. This

battle of blame regarding the breakup of the family goes on and on.

In Great Britain, women complain that the gulf between conventional images of family life and the reality of family life is enormous. What permeates governmental policy and advertising images is the ideal of the working husband and the homemaker wife at home with 2.4 children. One magazine claims that *less than 8 percent* of families in the United Kingdom actually fit that criteria!

Many women I have met feel that the nuclear family is a trap where they find themselves doing all the work. Now that there are more women who are both homemakers and breadwinners, they feel that men should share equally in the caretaking responsibilities.

In some cases women are deliberately choosing to raise children alone, and without guilt or shame. They are not desperate to get married, remarried, or whatever. On the contrary, singleness is a fact of life. Families headed by women are a fact of life. An Australian television show on the family interviewed people who were not in traditional nuclear families and who wanted to be very clear to the world that they *are* part of a family nonetheless. Having no father in residence does not negate them as a family.

The one question remaining is this: Can we accept this growing trend of diversity in families?

·103·

CREATING
SACRED
RELATIONSHIPS

COURAGE

It takes COURAGE to risk being in a relationship.

It takes COURAGE to be willing to change.

It takes COURAGE to be yourself all the time.

It takes COURAGE to always tell the truth.

It takes COURAGE to share all your feelings.

It takes COURAGE to rise above your conditioning.

It takes COURAGE to break out of a mold or a role.

It takes COURAGE to break family traditions.

It takes COURAGE to get out of a rut.

It takes COURAGE to try something new.

It takes COURAGE to look at your shadows.

It takes COURAGE to admit that you are wrong.

It takes COURAGE to take responsibility for your part in an upset.

It takes COURAGE to take responsibility, period.

It takes COURAGE to not blame others.

It takes COURAGE to give up an addiction.

It takes COURAGE to forgive a heartbreak.

It takes COURAGE to stay present with people.

It takes COURAGE to find solutions.

It takes COURAGE to see things differently.

It takes COURAGE to leave when you should leave a relationship.

It takes COURAGE to be alone and be happy.

It takes COURAGE to start over with your partner.

It takes COURAGE to start over with someone new.

It takes COURAGE to commit to healing your entire body.

It takes COURAGE to begin a spiritual mission.

It takes COURAGE to stay on a spiritual path.

It takes COURAGE to surrender to a spiritual teacher.

It takes COURAGE to be vulnerable.

It takes COURAGE to open your heart to a community.

It takes COURAGE to ask for support.

It takes COURAGE to be willing to be processed.

It takes COURAGE to receive feedback with a positive attitude.

It takes COURAGE to be totally diplomatic and supportive always.

It takes COURAGE to network.

It takes COURAGE to be rebirthed.

It takes COURAGE to go for what you really want.

It takes COURAGE to make a difference.

It takes COURAGE find your voice and to speak your truth.

It takes COURAGE to be in the forefront of change.

It takes COURAGE to make a stretch.

And it takes a lot of Courage to be an Immortal!

DO YOU HAVE IT? IF NOT, YOU CAN GET IT. ENCOURAGE EACH OTHER!

Now try reading the list again and substitute the word *self-esteem*.

ENCOURAGEMENT
AND GRATITUDE

•

THERE IS NOTHING NEW ABOUT THE QUALITIES OF encouragement and gratitude; but there may be a new way to use them in an enlightened relationship. Imagine this:

Early in a relationship, you decide to tell your mate about the issues you are working on at this time in your life. You ask your mate for his support and encouragement with this problem. You also promise to work on your problem with diligence. You are grateful for your mate's support. You do not feel threatened. You express this gratitude when you are getting encouragement and support. You also give your mate permission to point out to you unconscious backsliding on your part; furthermore, you are grateful to be awakened about that unconsciousness. Your mate always tries to be encouraging rather than critical by holding the thought in his mind that this block can be healed.

Sound impossible? Well, it isn't. This is happening more and more in our communities. In the beginning, we made mistakes. We were often at the mercy of our blind spots. We knew we needed feedback but we were still sometimes defensive about receiving it—and a bit critical in giving it. But we never gave up the model and it is improving all the time. We have learned that if you can analyze yourself fearlessly, you can stand the critical analysis of others without flinching. Also, as you give up defensiveness, feedback comes to you much more diplomatically and tenderly, with encouragement behind it. Defenses attract attack. Both of these lessons became evident simultaneously. By the time we mastered self-analysis, and it no longer mattered how someone expressed feedback, the wording of it had become much more encouraging anyway.

The level that those of us who have stuck with this process are reaching now is best described as a keen awareness of what our hang-ups are—and we do ask our mates and the community for support in coping with them. We are grateful. If we don't recognize our hang-ups and someone else does and points them out to us, we are even more grateful. We want to know how we are coming across. Try this attitude. Start now!

The old way of handling each other's hang-ups has been called "co-dependent bargaining." A couple had an unconscious "agreement" which went something like this: "I won't confront your heavy smoking habit if you won't make me confront my spending habits." There is mutual denial—no attempt on either side to encourage soul progress. In the New Paradigm, there is no room for these co-dependent maneuvers because they only leave you more stuck. The opposite of denial would be overkill (or dwelling too much) on your mate's faults. There should be an appropriate balance. Self-analysis is the key. Remember this quote from Yogananda: "Those who DWELL on faults of others are like human vultures" (Yogananda, 1982). That is why we recommend analyzing yourself and asking for support in the process. Practice encouragement. Everyone will feel like you are a friend, a helper.

I have been trying a new approach in my personal life. I try, as soon as I can, to have the *most* gratitude for that which upsets me the *most* about a companion. If it upsets me, it must really be a shadow I need to look for in myself.

DIVINE CONTROL

ARE YOU AFRAID OF LOSING CONTROL OR OF BEING CON-
trolled by others? If this possibility is in the forefront of
your mind, you can be sure you will attract it. You will
find somebody to control you so you can, in turn, resent
it. You will imagine that you are being controlled the
minute someone does anything remotely resembling a
parent or authority figure. Let's look at the *real* question
of control.

If you are out of control, then nobody can control
you. If you are in control, then you are trying to use your
ego to stop the flow of life, or the Holy Spirit, from roar-
ing through you. In this sense, it is harmful for you to be
in control, as you are using the Ego Mind against yourself
which causes pain, sickness, accident, or even death. In
rebirthing, if you stop the life force by hanging onto a
negative thought with power—you experience paralysis.
People believe that, if they let go, something terrible will
happen. But all that really happens is that you let go of
negative thoughts that would hurt you otherwise. If you
can let go of ego control, and accept that the Divine runs
everything, then you will experience an abundance of life,
energy, love, joy, and money!

When you meet a true guru, you do not think about
controlling him or her. You want to surrender instead. A
true guru, male or female, is totally guided by Divine
Control. He or she is completely in present time—completely there with you—completely conscious, alive, wild,
and connected to everything. This person is "God-intoxicated" and irresistible. You want to surrender and you

want to be like him or her. Often, you cannot tolerate staying in a guru's presence too long if you do *not* surrender. You confront your own unwillingness to be in present time, your own limitations, your own blocks, and negative addictions. So you stay as long as you can without going nuts. Later, you go back for more teaching and insight, hoping you can be more like your guru the next time. The guru teaches you Divine Control.

If two people can stay out of control together, it is bliss. It is ecstasy. Staying out of control requires that both totally surrender to Divine Control by giving up their ego-based addictions. This rarely happens at the same time, and when it does, it is mostly during sexual ecstasy; that is why people are addicted to sex. But what if you could be out of control *all of the time*? It is something to pray for. It is something to reach for as a goal in the New Paradigm.

Controlling someone with the use of anger or fear is not only manipulative, it misses the point spiritually. Manipulation, control, and anger have nothing to do with true power. True power is love, safety, and certainty. Someone who is certain about who he or she is, who is completely loving and safe can walk into a room and take over without even speaking. He or she doesn't want to take over, doesn't need to take over, he or she just *is* and that is enough. If you have yet met a Saint like this, you are very fortunate.

DIVINE LOVE

PLATO SAW LOVE AS A LADDER CONSISTING OF SEVEN steps ranging from love of an individual to love of the universe's highest realities. The bottom step is number one, as follows:

1. Falling in love with the quality of another's form.

2. Loving all beautiful, physical forms.

3. Loving the beauty of the mind, regardless of form.

4. Loving beautiful practices, such as ethics, fairness, justice, and kindness.

5. Developing a love of beautiful institutions such as family and society.

6. Developing a love of the universal and the abstract including the sciences, loving the whole cosmos.

7. Experiencing a love of the everlasting manifestation of beauty itself: The immortal Absolute.

Love is the highest energy known to man. Love and life itself are one. *A Course in Miracles* would say that we do not have to seek love; what we have to do is to remove blocks to the awareness of love's existence. We have to dismantle the blocks we have built against love.

We tend to make the love of a man or a woman our ultimate goal in life—which is very limiting. We are blind to the real goal of life which is to become intoxicated with Divine Love. Human love has the potential to be gradually transmuted to Divine Love. Relationships carried on only through the body can only end up in disaster and misery. They become what the Course calls "special hate relationships." Human love manifests itself at different levels depending on how entrenched one is in the ego. The lower forms of love can easily turn into hate. Meher Baba said that the lowest forms of love (i.e. infatuation, lust, and greed) are actually perverted forms of loving. But even the highest form of human love differs qualitatively from Divine Love.

Divine Love blooms when a person attains spiritual perfection. Divine Love can descend upon a human being by the grace of a perfect master or the Divine Mother herself when this being has been prepared spiritually. Supreme Divine Love arises once the individual human Ego Mind disappears. This occurs after lifetimes of spiritual purification or when the Perfect Master determines that the aspirant is ready. Where Divine Love is present, the person is God-intoxicated and irresistible. Shastriji, to whom I dedicated this book, manifests this state at all times. He possesses unbounded spontaneity. Divine Love is God. It is still possible to meet him!

The great masters in history were channelers of Divine Love. Think of Jesus. Think of Buddha. Babaji. They are our true models. The goal of every being must be Divine Love. It is not reserved for just a few. It is the ultimate destiny of all souls. Always remember that behind all human love is the spiritual love of God. Yogananda calls it "the romance of Divine Love" (Yogananda, 1982). The greatest romance is with the Infinite. If you are living with someone, seek the Divine together. Ask the Cosmic Divine Mother to purify you so that you can channel this Divine Love daily, and with deepest sincerity.

SURRENDER

WHEN YOU HEAR THE WORD "SURRENDER" YOU MIGHT imagine yourself having to give in to someone else's wishes or demands. But what I am actually referring to is more of a surrender of self—a surrender to one's Divine Self. A person suffers only because he or she is ignorant of his or her true being. We are ignorant because we believe that we are our ego. We are ignorant because we identify ourselves with our Ego Mind, body, and physical senses rather than with our True Reality, or Spirit (Atman). As long as we maintain this ignorance, we forget that God is within us and we feel empty. We want to find something to feel full again and we don't know what it is. We start craving things. We accumulate desires which involve us in a lot of action. We try everything in an attempt to find what we are seeking. We continue wanting to find something. This continuous craving and its related action involves us in even more binding karmas. Soon, we end up craving death!

To find real life, we must transcend the ego. The ego is the barrier to happiness and knowledge. You have to die the death of the ego to be reborn spiritually. This is the obstacle to overcome in spiritual life, whether you are Christian, Hindu, or Buddhist. The ego is the only obstacle to God Consciousness. So, what do you have to do? Surrender yourself. Give yourself up to God completely. Become absorbed in God. It sounds simple, but it is one of the hardest disciplines one can possibly undertake. You have to be vigilant against the ego. God is the only Reality. You have to know in your heart that God not only exists, but is attainable as well. You will not reach God by leaving the world. You get there by surrendering your ego to God every moment of your life (Sherwood, 1963, FIP, 1992).

In a relationship, each should assist the other in this goal of self-surrender. The problem is that "truth cannot deal with errors that you want." In other words, your mate, your teacher, or anyone else may be willing to help you see the truth, but if you do not want to let go of your ego's false beliefs, then nobody can help you.

What everyone must deal with, then, is an identity problem. People who are open to a New Paradigm must first have their identity straightened out. Example: If you think you are separate from God, you will feel weak, you will have fear, and you will have low self-esteem. The Course says, "Every decision you make stems from what you think you are, and represents the value you place on yourself. Only an illusion stands between you and the holy Self that you are" (FIP, 1992). The ego must be replaced by the Truth, which knows no separateness.

The Course tells you that in you is all of Heaven. All power is given unto you in earth and heaven; there is nothing that you cannot do. When you join with another in a holy relationship, you join in truth and detach yourself from the belief that your identity is ego. When you accept truth as the goal of your relationship, you become a giver of peace.

ESPECIALLY FOR WOMEN

IF YOU ANSWER YES TO ANY OF THE FOLLOWING QUES-
tions, this essay is *especially for you*:

1. Did you grow up always trying to please others?

2. Were you taught to obey authoritative, patriarchal truths?

3. Do you find it difficult to trust your self?

4. Do you feel that you cannot be effective in society unless you imitate a male model?

5. Do you compromise yourself around a man?

6. Do you give in and do anything to avoid his irritation?

7. Do you reorder your priorities to accommodate a man?

8. Do you allow yourself to be treated as a sex object?

9. Have you forgotten that you are actually an aspect of the Divine Mother?

Read what Barbara De Angeles says about the six biggest mistakes women make with men:

- Women act like mothers and treat their men like young children.

- Women sacrifice who they are and put themselves second in importance to the man they love.

- Women fall in love with a man's potential.

- Women cover up their excellence and competence.

- Women give up their power.

- Women act like little girls to get what they want from men.

(De Angelis, 1991)

When I led women's groups in the 70s, we sat around and talked about men and sex. It was fun but I would never do that now. In the early 90s I began helping women to raise their consciousness instead. I did this by processing them on their fear of being equals with men, and on their fear of being powerful. Women expressed actual terror that a man would leave if they were into their own power. Most had never even taken the risk to find out if it would happen—they just held themselves back.

Now I am working directly with the Divine Mother energy to help women feel safe in passing through this block. The results have been marvelous. The more spiritual I got with my approaches, the better they work. But I have noticed that the men have been feeling left out. They have started showing up for these evenings. I let them stay. I do not throw them out. One man invited me to speak at a men's group! I did all of the same spiritual things— Divine Mother Prayers and all! They loved it. The only addition was to interview men about why they are slow to attend seminars. They answered that they feared looking weak. Women, however, actually see men as strong when they go to seminars.

THE WHOLE WOMAN

THE WHOLE WOMAN KNOWS WHO SHE IS. SHE IS CLEAR that she is one with God. She is enlightened and therefore she is aware that her own thoughts produce her own results. She is not a victim and she does not blame men or anyone else. She is not angry at men or anyone else. She does not feel limited as a woman. She understands that she is not her ego, which is limitation itself. She lives in terms of her being instead of in terms of pleasing. She is true to her essence and her spiritual path, always.

The Whole Woman honors and trusts her intuition. She can express her intuitive ideas in such a way that others are excited to hear about them. She does not have to push or manipulate. She simply has enough self-esteem to express her intuitive ideas so that they are heard and appreciated. She does not feel held back by men because she does not allow them to hold her back. Her position is natural and non-threatening because it comes from her heart and her spirituality.

The Whole Woman holds her feminine and masculine sides in balance. She can easily stand up for herself and she is not afraid to be seen *and* heard. She can express her opinions fully and without hesitation. She enjoys being female and is totally comfortable with her sexuality.

The Whole Woman understands that she is an aspect of the Divine Mother. She knows she is not a sex object. She is loving, soft, nurturing, giving, compassionate, caring, vulnerable, and wonderful. She is also strong, productive, and always searches for the truth. Cooperativeness and peacefulness do not make her weak. She has high self-esteem and respect for herself always, whether she is at home with the children, in the workplace, or involved in both.

The Whole Woman will not sell out just to keep the peace. She will not tolerate sexism, male superiority, or sarcasm. But she does love men. She is not against them. Her goal is to raise the consciousness of herself, her loved ones, and all of society. She understands that she is capable of producing positive change on the planet. The Whole Woman is not afraid of her power; she does not feel that she is a threat to men. She attracts men who like and are excited by her wholeness and spirituality. She knows that her intelligence, love, spirituality, and sexuality are wonderful qualities and will attract wonderful people. She knows her feminine qualities are appreciated by all.

The Whole Woman is healthy because her mind is pure and she is an overflowing spring of aliveness. She is full of her magnificence and, because it is simply the truth, she displays no arrogance. She is all of these things whether or not she is with a man. She is all of these things whether or not she is a mother. She does not invalidate herself, because she understands her own value. The Whole Woman is someone people want to be with! She is an asset to all. The more total she is, the deeper she can go in her relationships; and the more intimacy she can sustain. The Whole Woman is not overwhelming. She is fun to be with! She is worth waiting for.

ESPECIALLY FOR MEN

IN INDIA, ALL THE GREAT GURUS, SADHUS, AND IMMORTAL Yogis (who are the most powerful men I have met in the world) surrender to and worship the Divine Mother. If you could travel to India with me to meet them, and *saw* this real power for yourself, you would reevaluate your idea of power. I honestly think you would want to be like them. And it is never too late for you to become a spiritual master. I salute any man reading this. Bless you. Where are you? Please let us know!

The spiritual master, Yogananda, said, "Every man who looks upon woman as an incarnation of the Divine Mother will find salvation." I think what he meant was that when you do this, as the God-realized masters have always done, universal love will come into your heart and you will be able to draw from women many spiritual treasures.

The most fabulous women I know are just craving liberated men. Women simply want to create their independence out of internal security; they do not *want* to fight with you.

In fact, we women want to co-create with you in a way that also turns you on! We don't want your real self to be different. We just want our relationship to change so we can also accept our spiritual responsibility for the planet—alongside you. We would like to work out a New Paradigm with you. Historically, there have been societies where women were honored and had very respected positions. They were not only honored as priestesses and oracles, they were included in leadership and there was true equality. It is starting to happen again—it is inevitable really. Soon, the new definition of power will include being able to handle an equal relationship! You can be sure of it. So why not start now? The paradigm of men and women as equals running society together is not only spiritually appropriate, it is also a turn on.

We would like to see more of you in seminars. They are great places to meet great women. Maybe that sounds corny, but I mean it in the sincerest sense. Socializing should not be the main purpose of a seminar, but it is a wonderful benefit.

Soon we will all become sick of the imbalance of power we see daily. Envy and hatred will become so bad we simply won't be able to stand it. Aren't we tired of suffering NOW? We all co-created this. If we can learn to be on the same side, to work together, we will all be winners; the children of the world will be winners, too. Supporting equal rights for women can release bad karma!

Believe it or not, after I wrote this, a friend called to say that her spiritual teacher had just told her that he is working with women a lot more now because, "women are the way for men to come home." He was talking about our real home, of course, going back to the Divine Mother. He is talking about merging with the higher love, the pure love, the Divine Love. It is through this Divine Love that we will, together, be able to tune into the Divine Plan for Humanity. The Divine Mother will teach us cooperation.

THE WHOLE MAN
BY BOB MANDEL

IN THE LAST TWO THOUSAND YEARS WE HAVE SEEN many role models for men. From the crusader to the Renaissance man, from the man in a uniform to the man in the gray flannel suit, from the explorer to the man of letters, the diverse images float through the contemporary man's mind like a multiple choice test for male correctness. In the last fifty years, we have witnessed the march of the male role models in a new form—the warrior, the wimp, and the wild man.

The warrior is really the old crusader fighting passionately for his belief system, be it a religion, a race, a nation, or a form of economics. This form of behavior is based on conquest and takeover. Whether it's the terrorist's blind faith in his cause, or the corporate raider engineering a hostile takeover, the model is clear: Vanquish the opposition no matter what.

In personal relationships the warrior is a total disaster. He perceives his partner as the opposition and devotes his energy to control and conquest. Maintaining power is his chief concern. He is constantly embroiled in conflict and debate. Female power is perceived as the ultimate threat of emotional truth over logical truth. Such a man is always in a holy war, needing total obedience to his way of thinking in order to feel secure. He is often violent in temperament, explosive in behavior, and any difference of opinion can trigger an abusive response. The warrior is insecure at the core, which explains his obsessive compulsive need to control his external environment in order to feel safe. He lives in constant fear of loss, and even winning brings only temporary satisfaction.

The spiritual warrior was, for a while, a popular alternative for men. This is the man who is on the side of spirit, engaged in the internal struggle for self-realization. He is often a loner, a man on a solitary path, searching the world within and the world without for signs of God's presence. The problem with this model is that it is still based on war. When this type of man enters an intimate relationship, his independent path is threatened by the prospect of commitment to another human being. He too falls into the holy war syndrome, protecting his need for separation in order to maintain the sanctity of his spirit. The spiritual warrior is also often in conflict with the entire material universe, viewing money, home, and any material possessions as a denial of spirit. His basic flaw is his perception that spirit and matter are separate. His basic behavior may be less violent than the physical warrior, but not necessarily. After all, every warrior sees himself as spiritual, with God on his side. The crusader is thinly disguised by the euphemistic spiritual warrior.

With the advent of the Women's Movement, many men became wimps. This "soft male" was a response both to fathers who were dominant warriors and mothers who were smothering nurturers. When the father began to disappear from the home, ceasing to participate in the raising of his sons, boys grew up in a female world, imitating their characteristics as well as what they desired in men. It seemed like the way to win female love was no longer to wear a uniform and conquer the enemy, but rather to be sensitive, compassionate, sweet, and gentle. The perception of a world brought to the brink of destruction by male control also contributed to men who no longer wanted the responsibility of authority.

The problem with the wimp is that he is a wimp. Even though his softness seems attractive at first, when women attempt to relate intimately to such a man they are often frustrated and disappointed. He may have many commendable qualities, he may have tapped into his female side, but he can be as emotionally inaccessible as his father was. He often doesn't even know what he feels, let alone how to express it. His emotional world has been stifled by inadequate male bonding and overwhelming female influence. He is unhappy, indecisive, helpless, powerless, empty, lonely, and angry without knowing it. The wimp is an overcompensation for the warrior, an extreme and unsatisfying reaction, who cannot fulfill himself, much less a powerful woman. When a liberated woman and a soft man try to have a relationship, the traditional roles become reversed, but the dynamic of power and control, conquest and subservience, continues.

The Wild Man Movement is a healthy response for men in recovery from warring and wimping out. Robert Bly's appeal to so many men in need of their male identities should not be surprising. A poet in touch with the rhythms of the earth, his call to men to gather for ceremonial rebirth fills a huge gap in the male psyche. Here, men can gather as men, talk about their feelings among themselves, and retrieve the lost, primitive parts of their initiation into malehood. They can beat their drums, pound the earth, chant their chants, and recapture the primal meaning of masculinity.

The problem is, what happens when the wild man comes back to his family? His male identity, so bruised and fragile, now recovering with fellow men, can be suspicious and unsafe with women. He has learned how to take care of his male needs with other men, a valuable lesson for sure, but can he bring his process of recovery into harmony with healthy, heterosexual relationships? Has his tribe become overly male? And has this tribe replaced his family as the prime source of nurturing? Men's groups, like women's groups, are wonderful vehicles for healing, but the healing process remains incomplete until men and women come back together, discovering the joy of unity.

Men and women are now crying out for new equality in relationships. For men, the challenge to become whole is now at hand. What is a Whole Man? First of all, he is wholly himself, unfragmented and at peace with his maleness as well as his femaleness. He is spiritually whole. He has made his peace with God, resolving his personal conflict with this supreme male image of power and authority. He no longer sees God as the ultimate absentee father, but rather as a presence within and without. The Whole Man is his own authority, the author of his life, but authority no longer wears the warrior's uniform. Nor is his authority based on separation and threatened by community. Looking within and seeing no lack, the Whole Man is complete, comfortable with both his sphere of influence and his sphere of surrender. He is pro-active, a man of action, a creative force to be reckoned with. But he is also a good listener, open to new ideas and external feedback. He is committed to the greatest good for the greatest number. He gives space rather than being territorial. He understands his emotions and has learned how to express them in a language that can be received by men and women alike. His wildness and his softness, his aggressiveness and his receptivity, are blended in successful behavior patterns.

The Whole Man wears no particular uniform because he knows that the clothes don't proclaim the man because his wholeness is not an image but a presence. He lives in the real world, embracing the spirit of business and the spirit of family with equal devotion. He respects his environment and feels a part of the larger whole. He is a visionary, an entrepreneur, a gardener, and a carpenter. In other words, he is not defined by his trade. His career is his course of life, his path, and he sees no separation between his spirituality and its physical form.

The Whole Man is a romantic but not hopelessly so. He is a romantic realist whose passion and love are grounded in truth and simplicity. He doesn't fall in love, he rises in love. And the people he loves, both men and women, are powerful, creative, expressive and, like himself, holy and whole.

"No man is an island, complete unto himself," wrote the poet John Donne. The Whole Man is well aware that his wholeness is interconnected with the wholeness of the universe. He has a natural sense of belonging, and his respect for all of life leads him to honor all the people he relates to.

Since he has no need for special attention, the Whole Man has only holy relationships. He is not egotistical but humbly feels that he is God's gift to the world and the world is God's gift to him.

A HEATED DISCUSSION

To my amazement, the very night I finished this book, I witnessed another intense debate between men and women. I went out to celebrate with a new friend who, in turn, brought along some of her friends. Most of the people seated at our table were totally new to me, which I enjoyed. I was seated next to a brilliant financial astrologer. He began to tell me all of the manipulative women he had been with; he seemed very discouraged. I began teasing him about the possibility of his being a forceps birth. He found this amazing as a psychic had told him that before. He became fascinated with my current writing. He told me that he thought women were losing their femininity because of the way they handled business. He was trying to say that women should not use the men's manual for doing business.

At this point, the other women at the table, some of whom were very successful in business, began to enter the conversation. They took offense to what he was saying, and actually became quite aggressive! He looked at me and said, "See, this is exactly what I am talking about!" A heated debate ensued; I tried to smooth things out. I kept interviewing this man. I asked him if he was willing to become involved with a woman equally as intelligent as he was. He said yes, but he did not want one who was competitive, aggressive, and angry as those were already very dominant male traits. Other men at the table jumped in and agreed with him. I told him I could hear this. I asked him to imagine how it would be if he could create a woman who was intellectually his equal, successful in business, feminine, without competition and aggression. His mind stopped. He could barely speak. I could see that he wanted it but he could not believe that such a woman was possible. I helped him change his expectations and his vision. Once he did, the women at the table also changed; they dropped their aggressive stance. This was very interesting to watch.

This, to me, was a microcosm of the situation at hand. Women think they have to be competitive and aggressive and "male" to make it in business. Men want women to be women, but have come to expect them to act like men in business. Both have to see things differently. Men do not like to see the parts of themselves that are angry and aggressive reflected back to them. This man was saying, in effect, "Be yourselves and show us men another way."

As an example of another way, this man felt that Asian businesswomen had learned how to succeed in business and do in it a feminine way and Western women had not. But everyone at the table seemed more interested in fighting about it rather than listening to each other and learning from each other. Let's hope this interaction changes!

Anyway, I learned a lot from this discussion. I encourage women to be themselves and to do business from the heart. I encourage men also to imagine and help create the space for women to try new models. Everyone should think about giving up aggression, competition, and anger. That is the real point.

LIFE ITSELF AS A MIRROR

EVERYTHING WE SEE, WE SEE THROUGH THE SCREEN OF our own mind. So when we look out into the universe, we are looking through a filter which contains all that has happened to us, all that we have learned, all that we have suppressed. If we look through a dirty one, we won't see the outside so clearly. If we think, "I am not good enough," we see everything as not good enough or we feel not good enough in comparison to what we see.

Enlightened people know that a relationship is a mirror. Their interpretation of what they see mirrors how they see themselves; the content of their own consciousness.

Everything is a mirror. Couples can have fun going out into the world to see what they will create. All of life becomes a kind of "Rorschach Test." At the end of a day, discuss this interesting feedback from the universe:

- "I got a parking ticket today."
  (How did I create that?)

- "The boss really disapproved of me today."
  (How did I create that?)

- "I lost everything in the computer today."
  (How did I create that?)

- "Nobody would pay any attention to what I was saying today."
  (How did I create that?)

- "Somebody stole the tape deck in our car today!"
  (How did I create that?)

- "I was an hour late to my appointment today because of long distance calls and my client was really mad."
  (How did I create that?)

- "The kids wrecked our neighbor's yard."
  (How did we create that?)

- "I got fired from my job and it does not seem fair."
  (But how did I create that?)

- "I just found out that somebody on my staff was embezzling money from my company; and I am absolutely furious."
  (But how did I create that?)

In the New Paradigm, a sensitive and enlightened mate helps his or her partner look at how he or she creates situations, without adding to his or her feeling of guilt. Together, they figure out how to turn the situation into a win. After they have done self-analysis to discover the consciousness factor that caused the situation, they clear it through spiritual purification techniques. Then there might be a real opportunity to clean it up so it won't happen again. For example, if you are laid off from your job, you might go back to your boss, confess your "case" and express what you learned from the situation. Who knows, the boss might give you another chance. But even if he doesn't, the relationship may be healed and the possibility of this happening again may be prevented. People fire themselves. There are no victims.

THE HIGHEST REALITY

THE HIGHEST REALITY IS THAT YOU ARE ONE WITH GOD, and your mate is one with God. God is life and love and bliss. Everything else is not real. Everything else is an illusion. Everything else is only as aspect of the ego and the ego is merely a fearful thought, a mistaken identity, a false self that we make up. The ego is the thought that you are separate from God. But you cannot really be separate from God.

Belief in the ego, however, causes you to experience separation; it makes you experience fear, guilt, pain, misery, struggle, conflict, worry, disease, depression, and death. The ego is just a belief. You can dispel it by withdrawing belief in it. It is only your allegiance to it that gives it any power.

When your mate is experiencing his limited mind (ego states listed above) you must be careful not to agree with his illusion about himself. See your mate as healed. See your mate as perfect, alive, loving, joyful, peaceful, and immortal (the Holy Spirit's mind). This is precisely how Jesus healed people: He refused to fall into step with their limited mind. He saw only the Holy Spirit in them; his reality was so clear and strong that, in his presence, people could not maintain their old reality.

However, when your mate is having a crisis, he believes it is real. He experiences fear, because the ego is fear and the fear seems real. We are addicted to the belief in the ego, and waking up to reality takes time. So it is best to give your mate the space to feel and to express and not cut him off. Gently remind your partner who he really is and what he really can do. This is the encouragement he needs. Encourage your mate to remember the Holy Spirit's mind.

As for all of the purifications and processes recommended in this book, their only purpose is for remembering and clearing away the illusions of veils which, in fact, are just cobwebs that cover up the real self—the God-realized self. Having a relationship of any kind helps us do this. "No one alone can judge the ego truly. Yet when two or more join together in searching for Truth, the ego can no longer defend its lack of content. Our union is therefore the way to renounce the ego in you. The truth is both of us is beyond the ego" (Vaughan and Walsh, 1992).

To understand the highest reality to the fullest, read *A Course in Miracles* completely. If you find it too difficult at first, you can refer to the study guide I have prepared called *Drinking the Divine*. This essay can be considered a small step toward understanding the Course, which is the real truth. If we could all stay in that paradigm, which is our true reality already, we would not need this book or any other book; there would exist no conflict in relationships.

However, until we reintegrate who we really are, we will have to do the best we can with where we are now. In the meantime, all we can do is invite in the Holy Spirit to our minds for correction of all our wrong thinking, and pray that our relationship be used for His purpose.

THE DIVINE MOTHER

•

SPIRIT AND DIVINE MOTHER ARE ONE. THE HOLY
Spirit sounds masculine, the Divine Mother sounds feminine. The reality is that God is both Father and Mother
—infinite wisdom and infinite feeling.

In India, they say that the Divine Mother is the origi-
nal spark of creation. We are talking about connecting to
the power of the atom (not to be mistaken with the Virgin
Mary, who is only one aspect of the Divine Mother). The
Divine Mother is the feminine aspect of God.

By repeating the names of the Divine Mother, one
can link up with the qualities of that force and embody
them. These names (which number 108) are written by
Shastriji and say more than I could ever say about who is
the Divine Mother. Here is but a sample:

Om I bow to her,

SHE WHO IS MOTHER OF THE UNIVERSE

SHE WHO IS DIVINE ENERGY

SHE WHO GIVES BIRTH TO ALL

SHE WHO IS BOUNDLESS MERCY

SHE WHO REMOVES THE TROUBLES OF
    THE UNIVERSE

SHE WHO SHOWERS THE NECTAR OF
    GRACE

SHE WHO REMOVES ALL PAIN

SHE WHO IS BEYOND ALL THINGS

SHE WHO IS THE GODDESS OF
PERFECTION

SHE WHO IS THE POWER OF THE
BEGINNING

SHE WHO IS THE INAUDIBLE SOUND

SHE WHO IS ENERGY EVERLASTING

SHE WHO SHOWERS THE NECTAR OF
LOVE

SHE WHOSE EVERY ORGAN IS THE
SOURCE OF LIGHT

SHE WHO IS THE POWER OF THE ORIGIN

SHE WHOSE BODY IS THE UNIVERSE

SHE WHO IS THE PRINCIPAL POWER

SHE WHO IS THE POWER OF OM

SHE WHO IS DIVINE SOUND AND LIGHT

SHE WHO IS THE MOTHER OF FIRE

SHE WHO IS THE EMBODIMENT OF
DIVINITY

SHE WHO GIVES NOURISHMENT AND
PLENTY

SHE WHO HEALS ALL WOUNDS

SHE WHO SHINES LIKE THE STARS

SHE WHO IS THE GIVEN OF ECSTASY

SHE WHO BLESSES THE WHOLE WORLD

SHE WHO IS AWE-INSPIRING

SHE WHO IS THE OBJECT OF MEDITATION

SHE WHO IS THE IDEAL OF NATIONS

Are you ready to soften your heart? Are you ready to be more affectionate to the children of the world and make the world safe for them? Are you ready to be more nurturing, kind, tender, cooperative, and encouraging in all your relationships? Are you ready to be filled with universal love and peace? Are you ready to love all the people of the world? If you are, the Divine Mother is ready for you. She will give you her Divine Love when you are ready.

THE DIVINE MOTHER MOVEMENT

THE DIVINE MOTHER MOVEMENT IS A MOVEMENT FOR both men and women, together. I don't know how to evaluate the Feminist Movement. Everyone knows, in some part of their being, that equal rights and equal opportunities are spiritually correct ideas. It seems like the word "feminist" got a bad rap (perhaps because of the anger associated with the movement.). Germaine Greer states that, "Despite its reputation, the women's movement just goes on and is the longest revolution." I agree even more with her statement that we have no idea what it might look like in the end . . . it is all part of the great unknown. What it might look like in the end is a movement of women and men, with the help and guidance of the Divine Mother, stamping out injustice together.

Germaine also reminds us that we don't know what a well woman looks like—whole and entire. Do we even know what a well man looks like? Each sex must become well, whole, and entire. How do we know what any whole being looks like? Well, that is why I go spend time with Saints every year, so I can see what that looks like; so I can feel it, experience it. The Divine Mother Herself is also teaching me.

Barbara Harrison commented that Germain had attempted years ago to teach us what a well, whole, and entire woman might be like. But then she gave up trying to show us that promised land, that fictitious shore. "And who will lead us now?" the author asks. Is this woman, in fact, fictitious? I don't think so. Maybe, just maybe, a whole woman has to be Immortal. Maybe a whole woman is one who becomes a God-realized Master. That should be the goal for us all really, men and women.

My gurus and the Immortal Yogis know this secret of surrendering to the Divine Mother. I have seen how they worship her. I am clear that they have been preparing me for this work for eons. Read my book, *Inner Communion*, to get a deeper look at the preparation I have had with the Divine Mother.

Every year I go to the Divine Mother Festival in the Himalayas. These visits are the most intense and rewarding experiences of my life. During this last particular visit, I participated in three major activations for the work of the Divine Mother Movement: In the Ganges River near the Divine Mother Temple (Dhuni) and in the Dhuni itself (the sacred fire temple dedicated to the Divine Mother, that my guru Babaji built himself at the lower ashram in the foothills); in the Divine Mother Festival at the Havan (elaborate sacred fire ceremony to the Divine Mother in the upper ashram); and in the most ancient Divine Mother Temple, Dranageri (over 5,000 years old where puja has been done every single day) higher up in the Himalayas. The last two ceremonies were done with Muniraj and Shastriji (pictured with me on the back cover), two of the purest men on earth who have surrendered to the Divine Mother.

AIMS AND IDEALS OF THE DIVINE MOTHER MOVEMENT

1. To surrender to the will of the Divine Mother and to the highest divine plan for humanity.

2. To embody the qualities of the Divine Mother in the self, daily life, and society.

3. To reach for joy, peace, health, abundance, and wholeness for all.

4. To encourage all souls to choose the path of spiritual enlightenment and liberation.

5. To liberate mankind from suffering, disease, and death.

6. To offer people a new life and proper methods of spiritual purification for release of obstacles.

7. To spiritualize the earth.

8. To encourage and achieve equanimity in relationships and to overcome domination and injustice. Specifically:

   a. To raise the consciousness of women and encourage leadership with men.

   b. To succeed in having men be comfortable and happy with these changes in society and relationships.

9. To demonstrate the magnificence of having equal couples run society together.

10. To teach people the glory of a life of service and immortality.

11. To constantly be empty vessels, willing to receive and manifest new thoughts, new paradigms, new relationships, new social structures, and new educational content.

12. To honor Babaji's teachings of truth, simplicity, and love; to build more temples to the Divine Mother across the earth.

OM NAMA SHIVAYA

Focusing on the Divine Mother now will soften our hearts. It will inspire us to be more affectionate to the children of the world and stimulate us to make the world safer for them. It will help us to feel more nurturing and more willing to solace the world with peace. It will fill us with more kindness, tenderness, cooperation, and encouragement in our relationships. It will fill us with universal love. Developing the motherly aspect of God will help us feel love for all people in the world.

CREATING
SACRED
RELATIONSHIPS

PRAYERS TO THE DIVINE MOTHER
BY SHASTRIJI

I AM PRINTING HERE JUST A FEW OF THE PRAYERS (excerpted from *Pure Joy*) by my beloved master, Shastriji, to whom I have dedicated this book. This will give you a sense of the true meaning of the Divine Mother. (Try reading these out loud.)

"Oh, Sivai, You are the embodiment of ultimate bliss and conscious Energy. You are supreme knowledge of the Absolute. You are the image of infinite compassion, unfathomable as in the deep sea. Oh Durga, Goddess of the universe, I prostrate before you."

"Oh Universal Mother, you give me shelter. In truth You are the one who gives life to all the beings of this world. You are the physician who cures the fever of the life and death cycles of the wheel of life. You are the source of life and liberation of all living beings. We pray to that timeless energy which resides as mother Goddess in Haidakhan. Remembering You is to crown this life with Success, to attain Liberation."

"Oh Mother, you are the embodiment of divine speech and hidden supreme knowledge. You reside in the temple of Lord Shiva's heart. The prayers of the Vedas are directed to Your divinity. You are the embodiment of the initial seed of 'OM' and are rooted therein. You are the Energy of Kundalini, giving birth to creation. The knowledge of You in this divine form enables the yogis no more to return to the Mother's womb."

"Oh, Goddess, who upholds the universe, You give perfection to all beings. To those who take refuge in You, You grant the most precious boons and give them happiness. We prostrate before you."

"You are adorned with a face that is luminous like the full moon. Your smile is tender and Your forehead is like a flawless mirror that reflects and issues divine light. It is said that he who meditates on the divine form of Her whose face shines like the full moon attains all happiness."

"Your Energy is beyond the power of even Bramah, Vishnu, and Maheesvara. Your form is eternal everlasting Peace. You are the root of all the elements. Oh Mother, you are mistress of the quality of goodness and of all other qualities. You are immortal."

If you were to meet Shastriji, you would feel like crying tears of joy. You would want to be like him and all other goals would pale by comparison. Shastriji is Babaji's high priest; he is an Ayurvedic doctor, a scholar, a prolific writer, a gifted speaker, a gifted clairvoyant, a gifted palmist, a saint, and poet in all lifetimes, is a rich businessman, and he is a totally God-realized Master. He has a happy marriage and healthy family. Shastriji has been reading prayers to the Divine Mother for over fifty straight years without fail—*Jai Maha Maya Ki Jai!* (Victory to the Divine Mother!)

Part Two:
Essays on Enlightened Business and Politics

KARMA YOGA

KARMA YOGA IS THE YOGA OF SELFLESS SERVICE. IT IS THE path for achieving Union with the Divine by shifting our awareness from self-preoccupation to that of serving the needs of others. To practice Karma Yoga, you do not necessarily have to change what you are doing. But you do have to look at your *attitude* about what you are doing. By dedicating our lives to serving others, we are working toward peace.

Karma Yoga purifies our heart and prepares us for the reception of Divine Light. It helps you attain the knowledge of God. It helps to clear past life karma. Because of our selfish actions in past lives, we have to keep reincarnating again and again. We are *bound*. Karma Yoga helps to liberate us from this cycle of bondage.

Because of the importance of Karma Yoga, I am writing a few essays in this section about business and the work place. Does it make any sense to try to have new paradigms at home in our relationships but not on the job? Of course not! Think about it: Are you really going to work on your personal relationship to end domination, and then go to work only to experience being dominated (or dominating) all day? We all want peace, harmony, joy, and equality in every area of our lives. Therefore, we cannot ignore business and the work place. We must apply enlightenment here as well. Business *is* relationships.

A Course in Miracles says that "The healing of God's Son is all the world is for." Therefore, our business life and work place is also for the healing of our ego-based mentality. We are here to replace the ego with the Holy Spirit's mind. That includes every moment. The Course would say that you should immediately turn your relationship over to the Holy Spirit for guidance. That applies to your business also. What if we placed everything we do in the hands of the Divine Mother? It is too easy to make the major mistake of separating work from our spiritual lives.

It may seem like new paradigms in business are simply returning to ancient spiritual truths. This is partially correct. However, elements of the "enlightenment movement" can also be added. Example: Rebirthing the whole staff together before a business meeting so that everyone is clear and can channel thoughts more quickly. This practice does not bring religious dogmas to the work place; it merely brings clear minds to support the business.

If you are an employer or supervisor and you offer new ideas, you will gain respect and loyalty from your staff. Who would not want to work for someone like this as opposed to one who uses fear tactics instead?

If you are an employee, you might think that you have no power to produce change in the workplace and that you have to put up with domination, manipulation, and aggression. That is not so. You, as an enlightened being working with the energy of the Divine Mother, can make a huge difference. The Divine Mother is love combined with power. You can inspire even authority figures to see things differently. Great bosses take feedback and welcome new ideas. If they are completely closed, maybe you should consider working somewhere else. But if you cannot leave the job right now, and you have a supervisor stuck in the old mentality, you might pray to the Divine Mother for help. An opportunity to mirror something back to this person may arise, and he or she will start to look at themselves in a different way.

BUSINESS AND SPIRITUALITY

THE MAJORITY OF PEOPLE TRY TO SEPARATE BUSINESS from spiritual life. This is a mistake. Since the purpose of life is to find God, then this purpose should be an integral part of any career. Otherwise, you could end up with a "hornet's nest of troubles," as Yogananda would say. Everyone has a role that he or she was designed to perform here. But, always, the essential part of that role is to put God and self-realization first in everything you do. So it is not as if you go to work and then come home and get enlightened in your free time. Your mandate is to use every single aspect of your life for the evolution of the Soul and for finding God. Every moment is a spiritual opportunity.

Once, in Sweden, I had the privilege of meeting the famous photographer, Lennart Nilsson, who took the first pictures of the fetus in the womb. To see him, I had to go to his lab, as he was always working. I followed him around and talked to him while he looked under microscopes. He asked me if I was writing anything about meditation. Suddenly he looked up at me and said, "Sondra, I am always in meditation." I could see that. His "God Contact" was constant and, as a result, he had become a total master of his trade.

You are among the Ministers of God, *A Course in Miracles* says. Your work is your ministry. Therefore, your ministry is everyone you meet, especially those in your address book, your workplace, and clients or customers that come to you. Marianne Williamson said once that your business is merely a "front" for a church! Another principle of *A Course in Miracles* is this: "The healing of

God's Son is all the world is for." Therefore, the world is here for your healing only. This means, of course, that your business is one of the main avenues for your spiritual healing, since you spend so much of your life there. If you are not tuned in to this potential, you are missing the main point of life. Your business is also for the spiritual healing of others who work with you. Those who choose to use business as part of their spiritual path will find that their labors are never in vain.

Your work should always be the highest service you can think of to mankind. Or, if you are not in a service type of career, figure out how to make your current business more service-oriented. This context is called Karma Yoga. The point is to put your whole mind into seeking God and serving humanity day and night, no matter which outward activities you are engaged in. You do this by seeing God in everyone and everything. You do this by using each moment to develop higher and higher spiritual qualities. You do this by disciplining yourself to give up anger, control, manipulation, greed, and corruption of all kinds.

BUSINESS, BALINESE STYLE

THE FIRST TIME I OBSERVED THE BALINESE PEOPLE AT work, I said out loud, "Dear God, what has happened to the Western world?" I was stunned. I was alone on the terrace having my first Balinese breakfast. Everyone had such a grace and holiness as they worked; it made me feel simply Divine. It seemed almost as if everyone was bowing to me and everyone else. Furthermore, there are temples everywhere in Bali. In addition, each home and place of business has its own active temple which is ceremoniously honored every day. The Balinese would never have a business without a temple or, at least, an altar on the premises.

The Balinese are very clear that no duties can be performed without receiving power from God. This power from God is honored daily and without fail. Before the Balinese people go to work, they do several hours of *puja*, or worship, to prepare themselves for the day. The family does this together. It is an incredible, sweet kind of meditation and worship. Of course, every home has a temple. The Balinese would never consider building a house without building a temple first. The house is built around the temple, which is the central core. Every day, rituals are performed. Worshippers weave beautiful, intricate, tiny straw baskets each day, in which they put flowers and food as offerings. They would never even consider going to work without this family worship to start the day.

The rice fields have their own temples; there are also local temples, and district temples. The ultimate temple is the Mother Temple on the top of a holy mountain which overlooks Bali. Next to that temple is a fascinating hall, open on all sides. This, I was told, is where the high priests meet to solve problems occurring in their society. Even major politicians have their homes right alongside the more important temples of Bali. Politics, business, and spirituality are all one. When you experience this, it feels absolutely right and wonderful.

The Balinese work in a very spiritual, focused manner. They literally become masters at what they do, whether it be making stoneware, basket weaving, woodcarving, silversmithing, painting batik, or being a simple shopkeeper. . . The work is an aspect of their devotion.

Elaborate, beautiful, and holy ceremonies are practiced regularly. There is worship to the Divine Mother specifically for businesses or families and even a special prayer day for cars and machines! One result of all this holiness is that the Balinese people are never overweight. This alone is interesting. Nor are they angry or stuck in competition. Everyone cooperates. To me, the Balinese have mastered a life of perfect action: There is a proper balance between the material and the spiritual because they know that their separation is not real.

Bali changed my life. I wish everyone would make a pilgrimage to this "island of the Gods." When I came home from Bali, I immediately made an altar in every room of my flat. I also began traveling with an altar. Now, I always make an altar in my hotel room and in the rooms where I speak and teach.

·

NEW MANAGEMENT

·

Did you know that traditional business hierarchies were originally modeled after the military? A rigid command structure was thought to provide the greatest degree of control for the leader. Today, however, hierarchies are being discouraged. Hierarchies in the corporate structure are crumbling. The centralized pyramid structure is being disassembled. Many of the layers of management between the top and bottom are also being eliminated, resulting in less separation between the managers and the managed—and this is good.

In my own organization, we have tried to be close to our staff members and to encourage them to be as clear as possible. Over the years, they had become so strong that they wanted independence from central headquarters. This desire could have been threatening to us, but we gave it to them. Initially, independence was a shock, and the transition was difficult for them. But everyone got on their feet and the whole organization was revamped. I felt it was time to delegate and move on. I found it very hard to let go, but I did so with the knowledge that I had created a viable, international organization that would continue to operate. A founder or owner is never out of a job. He or she is creative enough to become the founder or owner of something new for the world again and again. This is growth. This is expansion. This is life. This is exciting. Why make only one contribution to society?

The most successful examples in business are those in which the leaders consciously attract equals to work with them. Instead of fearing an equal, they thrive on the excitement and synergy generated by the relationship.

Management by fear is the old paradigm and causes nothing but stress and strain. Team management is both fun and rewarding, and there is an art to it: The art of cooperation.

CREATING
SACRED
RELATIONSHIPS

RELATIONSHIPS
IN THE WORKPLACE

SINCE WE ARE HERE TO REMOVE BLOCKS TO EXPERIENC-
ing love, then relationships are fundamental. People tend
to apply this principle only to their social and personal
lives, but it is just as relevant to our relationships in the
workplace. We say that the person who upsets you the
most is your "guru" or teacher. This is especially true at
work. Our worst relationships show us something in our
subconscious that we need to look at; they trigger our
fears. That is why these relationships are important
opportunities. If our boss or co-worker does not seem to
value what we say, they reflect the part of us that fears we
do not matter as well.

Relationships are assignments. Everyone you work or
meet with is an assignment you have given yourself. If
they mistreat you, you need to find out why you attract
this behavior. You do *not* need to forgive them for the
horrible thing they have done or take pride in your placa-
bility. That is the old idea of forgiveness. An appropriate
idea, in the New Paradigm, is the explanation of forgiveness given in *A Course of Miracle*s: Real forgiveness means
you have understood that you were *not* unfairly treated.
You attracted that behavior. You wanted it. Also, you are
not justified to attack in return. THIS IS BECAUSE ALL
OFFENSIVE BEHAVIOR IS REALLY ASKING FOR LOVE.
*A Course in Miracle*s says, "Every loving thought is true, all
else is an appeal for help or healing" (FIP, 1992).
Remember, when someone at work is not being loving,
they are asking for love.

The best book to read about applying *A Course in Miracles* to business is *In the Spirit of Business*, by Robert Roskind. The key lies in how we apply *A Course in Miracles* to our lives. I want to inspire everyone to read this book. In the chapter entitled "How Does the World Work," Roskind explains three main views people operate from:

1. No creator/random universe and planet

2. Created universe/punitive or indifferent planet

3. Created universe/benevolent creator and planet

Someone who operates from the first mind-set, feels the effect of everything and operates from victim consciousness. They believe in good or bad luck. They often feel helpless and out of control.

Someone from the second mind-set often experiences pain and suffering, and thinks they deserve it and you deserve it. They think sin is real and punishment is coming. Due to false religious theology, this mind-set is the most common.

Hopefully, you will gravitate toward those who operate in the third mind-set. This is the framework of *A Course in Miracles* and is needed for a new paradigm. These individuals know that they are the cause for the situations created in their lives; they do not believe in blame. These people see the universe as loving and safe. Nothing is an accident. Everything is a lesson.

HARMONY BETWEEN
INTELLECT AND INTUITION

IF A PERSON TRULY UNDERSTANDS THAT THE PURPOSE OF life is to find God, and that the purpose of the world is to heal God's Son, then business itself will take on a new meaning. Once a spiritual understanding of the deeper meaning of business becomes clear, it becomes possible to achieve balance between mind and heart, intellect and intuition.

The first thing to realize is that we should all be working toward this balance within ourselves. The Divine Mother energy is pouring through the planet now in a magnitude of ways. Men are becoming more intuitive, and women are speaking out more than ever before. Men and women are beginning to work together more closely; they have a real desire to do so. The mind and heart are no longer being pitted against each other in this new energy. Antagonism simply does not work. Therefore, men and women are learning cooperation. As this happens, it is becoming more and more desirable to have balance between the sexes in business. Justice between the sexes is not only becoming desirable, more and more, it is becoming required in the workplace.

To find spiritual value in the business world can be difficult. It is tempting to focus only on achieving material success. Compromising your integrity, whether spiritual or professional (they are the same), can eventually lead to manipulation and corruption, which causes guilt; and guilt demands punishment. At this point, your business may fail because of a backlash of karma.

When integrity is maintained at all times, your business will flourish. Prosperity consciousness is also important. When the heart and intuition (both are feminine aspects) are allowed to participate in a business, prosperity consciousness pours into the void left by the departure of the old model of poverty consciousness. Leading with the heart means leading with honesty.

I think we all want spirituality, vitality, and love in our work, with the maximum opportunity for everyone to grow. This is certainly more nourishing than the momentary surface "thrill" of financial power. It may be hard to make the shift at first, but it has to happen, so, don't delay. To be safe, and to avoid creating karma, always turn your business over to the Holy Spirit and the Divine Mother. We all need to help raise the vibration of the money systems up into the heart chakra.

CREATING
SACRED
RELATIONSHIPS

KEEPING EMPLOYEES,
STAFF, AND CLIENTS HAPPY

IT IS VERY IMPORTANT TO CREATE MEANING FOR THOSE who work for you or those who solicit your services. Whether they are employees, partners, suppliers, bankers, consultants, or even clients and customers, give them all the sense that they are doing something that makes a meaningful difference to you. And make sure you are making a meaningful difference to them. If you can add to the beauty of their life and the spiritual advancement of their soul, you will awaken a higher level of commitment and return.

Every really good book on business that I have read has emphasized the importance of listening to the employees; making sure they feel heard and really paying attention to their feedback. Implementing their ideas and giving appropriate recognition is also a good idea as is public acknowledgment of their contributions.

In addition, offering the staff growth seminars creates a lot of enthusiasm. Employees get the chance they deserve for spiritual advancement right in the workplace. In Australia, the government passed a law that required all companies to set aside a certain percentage of funds for in-service education, for raising the consciousness of Australian business. Why not offer staff courses in success consciousness, money management, and consciousness raising? It is simply common sense.

In the little town in Iowa where I grew up, I carefully studied the local businesses. There was only one commercial street. The busiest shops were those where people were allowed to hang out, chat, gossip, and sit by the fire.

The shops that did not foster warm relationships did not do as well. It was a real simple lesson to learn: If you make your business a place that is welcoming, workers will want to go to work and customers will love to visit.

As an adult, I think of the places I have loved to shop and I see the same principles at work. What was the special ingredient? What was the hidden X factor? Each of these business had a special feeling that permeated everything, and which had a lot to do with the conscious-ness of the owner. There was also the networking aspect. Take a simple example: The owner of a beauty shop in San Francisco was a natural networker. She would gladly put you together with another client you might like to know. I was new in town and she said to me, "You would really like X." We met and pronto, I had a new girlfriend! This girlfriend introduced me to what was going on in San Francisco in the consciousness movement. I could drop by this beauty shop any time and leave feeling uplifted—guaranteed.

How can you make your workplace more inviting? How can you make each customer feel like they are your most valued client? This is what "minding your business" should really mean.

ᴀLIGNMENT ON PURPOSE

ONCE I ATTENDED AN ENLIGHTENED BUSINESS SCHOOL for entrepreneurs. The teacher refused to begin the real program until we were all aligned with the purpose of the program. He would not begin until we had all agreed on every word of that purpose. This took four grueling days, but I understood his point: Aligning all employees is very important. Coca Cola did it. Their motto was, "A coke always within reach." They got everyone to align with this goal. The public is now trained to believe it is easy to get a Coke, close by, no matter where you are in the world.

I recommend that you build more spiritual goals into the purpose of your business, both personal and universal. I recommend that you teach employees the true purpose of business: To learn unconditional love and to become enlightened. Everyone can agree to use the marketplace as a testing ground for learning how to love each other more and how to commit to each other's evolution (e.g., between staff and employees, employees and other employees, employees and the customer, and the company and the community). If everyone can agree to this game plan, you will see a shift happen; a new vitality will take over the whole company.

More and more companies are committing to help with community and environmental issues that concern us all. These companies are becoming more spiritually inclined, whether they actually use the term or not. Anita Roddick of The Body Shop is being asked to speak to companies all over the world, which is very encouraging. This is not only spiritually correct, it is absolutely wise. When employees know that part of their efforts are spent in serving humanity, they feel much better about themselves and the company. If you know your company is aligned with environmental concerns, the welfare of society, plus your own spiritual enlightenment, you feel more like going to work. The practice seems obvious, but how many owners of companies are actually doing it?

Teaching people what it feels like to share a mission could be one of the most important things you do. People want a mission. They need one. They crave one. (Many dictators, benevolent and otherwise, have known this.) What we need to do now is to find a mission that is dedicated to life itself; for the good of all countries. Do you want your company to thrive and your employees to be happy? Then pay attention to whether or not you are vigilant in your quest. Why do people who joined the Peace Corps say it was the highlight of their lives? You already know the answer.

I just recently reminded my staff again, in a newsletter about our own task, which is to make people conscious of their divinity. I thanked them for remembering that there was no greater task on earth.

PROVIDING A SAFE PLACE
FOR SHARING

DOES THE PREVIOUS CHAPTER SOUND TOO GOOD TO BE true? Perhaps you work for the government or the military. Don't let that stop you. When I was a military nurse, I never hesitated to tell the top brass what was happening on the base that was unfair or unethical. For example, there was a big ruckus between the nurses over the issue of abortion. Things got so bad that I went to the colonel and insisted that a meeting be called for the nurses to share their feelings. This was done and everyone benefited. I found out that even the military would allow sharing between employees. I was not a rebirther then, nor an enlightened person. But I had a natural intuition to push for communication and integrity and I convinced this normally conservative hierarchy to create the space for it.

I recommend that a special time be set aside every week for sharing between staff members. When people are allowed to vent their feelings, they are happier and more productive. A memo system is good for those employees who have a fear of verbal feedback. The employees and staff can usually solve any problem so long as matters are not kept hidden. Trying to hide problems is futile anyway, because people are so psychic that they often sense a crisis, and gossip is inevitable. Many companies spend a fortune hiring outside consultants when it is not even necessary.

Everyone knows everything in our organization. We have nothing to hide. I personally welcome verbal feedback. I think it is stimulating; it helps me to improve relationships.

I have spent years studying relationships, group processes, communication patterns, and cooperation issues. I have studied how family patterns and ego-based thoughts can ruin a business. Applying enlightenment to any business problem is fun and rewarding. When there is a serious mistake, turn it into a learning situation. Punishment usually creates more tension and a tense staff is more prone to making mistakes.

In our business, we process staff members to find the consciousness factor that caused them to make the mistake. We apply the principles in the trainings and in the books I have written. This means that a supervisor or leader agrees before accepting the job, to be willing to try self-analysis in order to improve performance in the workplace. Everyone in the company understands that this is part of the job. If introduced properly into your company policy, this alignment gives your employees the benefit of spiritual enlightenment along with their salary. This is the way to create lasting job satisfaction.

Consider having one or two rebirthers on the staff of your business. Try it. They may handle emotional personal issues quickly and effectively, thereby contributing to the overall success of your organization.

ENLIGHTENED BUSINESS MEETINGS

I USED TO HATE BUSINESS MEETINGS. SINCE I HAD SO many strong personalities on staff, who I encouraged to speak up, I got a *lot* of opinions. It would sometimes take days to hash things out. I wanted them to be included in the decision-making process, but I did not want to get bogged down—and I did not like arguments.

Then I remembered to apply my own game, the Highest Spiritual Thought Game. We teach this game in the relationships trainings and I have mentioned it briefly earlier in this book. Let's take a typical meeting: There is an agenda. One agenda item is described as "Schedule," for example. The leader of the meeting states the topic, and/or the problem out loud. He or she encourages discussion in the following manner: Each person states what he thinks the highest thought is to solve the issue; they go around the room clockwise. The idea is to go for solution, go for resolution. Everyone must have this goal in mind and must have agreed to play the game. Anyone who has a higher thought speaks in turn. You may pass if you think the higher thought was expressed by the person before you. But someone on the other side of the table might channel a much higher thought. When the highest thought is out on the table, there is no more discussion, no more time wasted. You go immediately to the next agenda item.

One can tell if the highest thought has arisen because everyone agrees that it is the most positive, the most loving, the most productive, and it feels the best in each person's body. If there are two thoughts that are so close that the group cannot decide, a break is in order. During the break, people continue to discuss how they feel in small groups. If that does not work, meditation is in order. If the group is truly committed to this process they ask the Divine Mother for guidance; usually someone in the group will have a clear vision and the answer will become obvious. This game goes very smoothly if people breathe well, and if they are not stuck in their own process of anger or competition. If one person's energy is blocking the game from working, the group may have to stop and process that person. This can be done simply by saying: "_____, I want you to should share how you are feeling right now; you seem blocked." If more than one member is stuck, maybe the whole group needs to share. We often start out business meetings by sharing first. Often, when we have tried to take a short-cut and leave the group-sharing step, we have had to eventually back up and do it anyway. So I do recommend sharing as standard practice.

Once I had a meeting which got so stuck that I finally told everyone that the only hope for us was to lie down and rebirth ourselves together. So we did. The conference table took up nearly the whole room, so I told everyone to take away the chairs and lie with their feet under the conference table with heads sticking out. We all did this and rebirthed ourselves together for forty-five minutes. Then we got up and carried on the business at hand with no problem at all.

COOPERATION

ALL OF MY RECOMMENDATIONS TAKE COOPERATION, which sounds like a nice idea, but experience shows that it does not happen easily unless one has processed sibling rivalry and competition first. In business, especially, you often deal with "the invisible sibling syndrome." People tend to set up other workers as a sibling to be jealous of; the resulting unconscious competition can become deadly to the well-being of an organization. Some people believe that competition is healthy. They should read *The Case Against Competition* for an opposing viewpoint. We find cooperation, not competition, produces more creativity, joy, and synergy.

The business world is based on the concept of competition. But competitive systems are inefficient and archaic. As Robert Roskind so aptly states in his book *In the Spirit of Business*, "Competition will never allow us to view other people correctly. They must always be viewed as separate from us, as someone to be defeated and conquered. The real motivator that underlies it is fear" (Roskind, 1993). He adds that fear, as a motivator, depletes us. He asks if anyone can be considered a real winner if their prize is a greater sense of separation and alienation and a false sense of superiority over their peers. Cooperation encourages a view of others as equals and helpers in our goals. Cooperation allows truth to enter any situation.

A few years ago, I started thinking about how to solve the problem of competition in our organization. I developed a training program called Cooperation Training. However, it proved to be very difficult to get it organized —the assistants did not want to cooperate to organize it!

This was a shock to me, so I asked them to describe for me their idea of cooperation. They thought cooperation was basically doing what someone else wanted them to do. What a misconception! So, first I had to show them a true model of cooperation. I asked everyone to write a letter to the sibling they hated. Then I asked them to read it in front of the group. Some people had not spoken to their brothers or sisters in fourteen years! At one point, during the reading of the letters, everyone in the room started to cry. I had to stop the training and ask everyone lie down and get rebirthed right then and there.

Cooperation is exciting; it is all about synergy and creativity. People who work together on a mission, who want to make something happen, find it inspiring.

Once, I was on a basketball team that won thirty-four straight games. We had learned cooperation. You can always find employees and colleagues who have had this kind of team sports background. They can help transform a workplace into a cooperative mode. Keep in mind that some people are afraid of teams because the first team they ever encountered was a "delivery team." You would be surprised how much everyone's birth traumas affect business!

KNOWLEDGE OF BIRTH
AND BUSINESS

·

YOU MAY BELIEVE THAT BIRTH HAS NOTHING TO DO WITH business, but please read further. Think about the employee who is very valuable except that he is always late and this drives you nuts. Maybe he was born late. How about the employee who is great, and you need her, but she can't complete things? Maybe she was born Cesarean. What about the employee who does things backwards? Maybe he was born breech. Do you have an employee you really need, but everyone complains to you about his anger? Maybe he was forceps. How about the employee who cannot seem to come out of her shell? Maybe she was in an incubator or held back at birth. What about the employee who is a drain on everyone's energy, who sabotages everything? Maybe he needed a transfusion at birth. And finally, think about your own birth and how it may affect your business. You could literally turn it around if you clear your birth trauma. (For more information, refer to my earlier book, *Birth and Relationships*, also published by Celestial Arts.)

Furthermore, if you are the boss, owner, or manager, your employees may set you up as "the obstetrician" and thus become afraid and resistant in your presence. They may become so afraid that they cannot hear you. I give you over twenty years of research in *Birth and Relationships*, which can help you to help your employees and, therefore, your business.

The main factor that can affect business generally are the subconscious thoughts you form about yourself when you are born. These preverbal thoughts are called personal lies. Thoughts produce results; if you are not in touch with the heavy negative thoughts in your own subconscious, they can destroy your business and you may not even know it. Add to your own thoughts the subconscious personal lies of your co-workers or employees and imagine the potential for problems! Here are some examples of the thoughts I am talking about (remember subconscious thoughts also produce results):

I AM NOT GOOD ENOUGH

I AM A FAILURE

I AM BAD

I AM GUILTY

I AM EVIL

I AM NOT WANTED

I AM A MISTAKE

I AM TOO SLOW

I AM A FAKE

I AM WRONG

I AM NOT PERFECT

I AM STUCK

I AM UNLOVABLE

I AM A FAILURE

I AM NOT WANTED

I AM THE WRONG ONE

I AM A DISAPPOINTMENT

I AM NOT READY

I AM TOO MUCH

I AM DANGEROUS

These are some of the most common personal lies we encounter in rebirthing. I have written about how these thoughts affect your relationships in my other books. One of these thoughts may dominate your consciousness and cause you to act it out or pretend the opposite. These thoughts are usually unconscious until you are rebirthed.

Imagine if you had an unconscious thought, I am a failure, but you were desperately trying to succeed in business. No wonder it is not working. Can you now see what rebirthing can do for you and your company? These thoughts need to be not only changed, they need to be breathed out of the body.

RELATIONSHIPS TO THE
MATERIAL WORLD

ACCORDING TO THE MASTERS, SPIRIT ALWAYS HAS
supremacy over matter, but this does not mean you
should reject or avoid matter. Learn to use it as an expression of the spirit. Meher Baba said, "All the material
things of the world can be made subservient to the divine
game" (Meher Baba, 1988). He said that material things
in themselves are not good or bad, but their value depends
on the part they play in the life of the Spirit. That is, they
become good or bad, according to whether they help or
hinder the manifestation of divinity through them
(Meher Baba, 1987).

When we remember who we really are, and free ourselves of constant cravings, then we can have material
things and not get caught up in them. We use them, they
do not use us. A perfected person does not ignore things
of beauty nor hide in a cave to avoid the material world.
True spirituality is total. What matters is how a thing is
used.

Meher Baba says that detachment does not mean
coldness nor does it mean lack of appreciation. Detachment exposes to one the true values of material things.
Therefore, if I am detached, I am free of obsession, depen-
dence, and craving. I experience true understanding and
clear evaluation by being detached. The Masters would
say that if you are buried in matter, through life after life,
and forget that you are a soul, you punish yourself merci-
lessly. It just gets too hard.

If you get mixed up and start doing things which are
out of integrity to make more money for material things,

you jeopardize the progress of the soul. Corruption and the misuse of power will only bind the soul and cause a serious setback, which can lead to spiritual ruin. In the money seminars that I teach, I ask people to write down every single thing in which they are out of integrity: Lies told, cheating, not paying taxes, stealing, or even letting people down. Even minor things must be included such as using a phone a someone's house and making a long distance call without paying them back. These "insignificant" acts create new karmas too. I show people how to clean up each deed, one by one, until they experience being in total integrity.

Try to focus on the spiritual quality of total integrity instead of focusing on material goods, and see what happens in your life. Meher Baba observed that "Worldly people are so immersed in material cravings that nothing interests them unless it has some direct bearing on the fulfillment of these cravings" (Meher Baba, 1987). If you are in that category as a business person, you need to awaken to the fact that you are heading down the wrong path. The path you are on is a diversion which will interfere with spiritual progress. This does not mean that you have to give up money, but sooner or later you must reevaluate your priorities. It is never too late for repentance, reevaluation, restructuring, and rejuvenation.

INTEGRITY

IN BUSINESS, THERE ARE MANY OPPORTUNITIES WE MUST face which have the potential to compromise our integrity. Even though we know in our hearts that these temptations are against our moral standards, it is easy to rationalize doing them out by saying they are just normal ways of doing business. This rationalization is so easy that we often do not realize that we are being tested spiritually. A situation may seem insignificant, but there is no escape from the karma and no escape from the negative effects on the mind and body.

Every time we do something that lacks integrity, we experience guilt, whether we are aware of it or not. When you feel guilt, consciously or unconsciously, guilt demands punishment. So, we will invent ways to punish ourselves. All of us intuitively know what is right, just, and ethical.

In his book *In The Spirit of Business*, Robert Roskind points out that the temptations and tests that we create for ourselves in this area have to do with learning to choose love over fear. He says, "The greater the fear, the more intense the situation will appear, with major ramifications for many involved" (Roskind, 1993). He points out that fear and the ego will make a tremendous effort to convince us that it is valid to go against our better judgment. But even if we become "successful" by compromising our integrity, pain inevitably follows from this fear-based behavior.

Not long after I founded the Loving Relationships Training, I had a very big test. I hired a female business consultant who was quite famous. During the first board meeting she presented us with a "side business deal" in multimarketing. She was such a good salesperson that she could sell the socks off of anyone. Although I did not feel good about her deal at all, I watched her hook everyone, one by one, throughout the day. I noticed that the company cat kept jumping on her and wanting to scratch her. This added to my suspicion. When the group pressured me to sign the deal with this woman, I said "NO WAY!" The pressure my colleagues exerted on me was just incredible. One of my co-trainers and best friends was the most intense. I feared losing him over this. Finally I said, "It just so happens this yogi is in town. I am willing to sit down and go through this contract with him." At the end of that process, the yogi looked at my best friend and said, "If Sondra had said yes to this deal, it would have ruined your whole business." I no longer need yogis to help me say no, but I was glad for the help then.

What if your mate or your boss wants you to lie for them? It is an important spiritual test. It is bad karma for you to collude with another's poor ethics only because he or she is your mate or boss. You *know* this. Robert Roskind says we must ask ourselves, "What is the most loving course of action? and what will assist in removing the illusions?" (Roskind, 1993).

GRACE AND HUMILITY
IN BUSINESS

IF IT SEEMS LIKE THE NEW PARADIGM IS SIMPLY A RETURN
to ancient spiritual truths, it is. Some things should
always remain the same such as eternal truths and honor-
ing the commandments. The first commandment, for
example, means "don't replace God." The ego is a replace-
ment for God. The ego is idolatry. The ego is a false self
that we invent to replace God.

Aldous Huxley wrote an incredible essay on idolatry
which applies to business and is important food for
thought. He describes "civilized forms of idolatry" as
"belief in, and worship of human creation as though it
were God" (Isherwood, 1963). Education can increase
the attractiveness of higher forms of idolatry. In techno-
logical idolatry, devotees believe that their redemption
and liberation depends upon material objects, namely
machines and gadgets. This "religion" has its doctrines
spread all over the media, from which millions of men,
women, and children get their philosophies. He reminds
us that in Greece, when men and societies became exces-
sive, this gluttony had to be paid for. But today, techno-
logical idolaters don't believe they have to pay for their
craving.

Huxley describes political idolaters as substituting
spiritual truths with the worship of social and economic
organizations. The fanatic, he points out, worships something that is the creation of his own desires.

Even moral idolaters have to watch out or they will
worship their own ideals instead of God. When you give
up your own self-will and abandon yourself to the will of

God, Grace is given to you. With grace, our emptiness is filled.

Think about grace influencing your career. Where there is grace, there is no room for anger. Anger is connected to an overstressed or strong sense of ego, expectations, attachments, or thwarted will. If anger occurs, cleaning out the debris in the mind is needed. To consciously connect every thought and every single act of your life directly with the Divine helps you to rise above such impulses. To think about the Grace of Infinite Presence, which is available moment by moment, creates purity in your business life.

Finally, Huxley states that the more there is of the self, the less there is of the God Head. He says the law that must be followed is the Tao or the Way, which is that of humility and love. Huxley observes that, because people like their egos, they get a bigger kick out of bullying and self-adulation than they do out of humility and compassion. This attachment inevitably leads to wars, tyranny, and disease. Historically, men have preferred disasters instead of seeking the kingdom of God. Well, how about YOU?

Einstein once said, "I want only the thoughts of God."

EQUALITY IN THE WORKPLACE AND POLITICS

CONSIDER THIS: ACCORDING TO THE UNITED NATIONS, in one thousand years women will have the same economic and political clout as men (March 1994). The author of this article claims that it is ridiculous to expect favors from men in power because they are not concerned with critical issues such as anti-discrimination, child care, or equal pay. Women have to stand up for what they need, and men have to be more open. This will happen. It is dehumanizing and totally outmoded for women to cling to the belief that they are powerless to solve these critical issues themselves.

The author of this same article urges women to seek political power now. Otherwise, if the United Nations is correct, women will be waiting until the year 2994! But beware that the men who dominate the political system often make it difficult for women to get elected.

It seems clear to me that women will no longer put up with this situation. Women want to have the chance to influence the world as men do. Women *will* stand up, but they will leave behind the stereotyped feminism of the past. They don't want bitterness; they want cooperation. Former feminists want men to be involved with their process. The Divine Mother will also move so that the change is inevitable. Therefore, the businessman and politician who accepts this and who honors powerful women and equal rights, will be blessed again and again. Not only that, he will win the respect of all women. Any man who honors women's credibility is a powerful man, and is also a spiritually correct man. The universe will recognize him for that.

Take the chance in your workplace—whether you are male or female—to set the wheels in motion for professional equality. Encourage discussion between co-workers. Having everyone's interests at heart will improve your work environment. In Australia, *New Woman* magazine had a contest to determine which ad agency could come up with a creative way to sell feminism. The best one, by far, was from DDB Needham: The ad said, "EQUALISM, NOT FEMINISM" implying that, if you say the word *feminism*, you alienate the very gender whose support you need.

SPIRITUALIZED POLITICS

AN AUSTRALIAN WOMAN WROTE ABOUT WHAT SHE thought would make Australia a more "clever country." She observed that communication between the sexes could be much better, but she felt discouraged since men and women seem to see things so differently. She then proposed that the best way to facilitate communication would be to utilize the vision of both. She suggested that the Constitution be changed to have equal numbers of men and women in every chamber in Parliament in Australia. A citizen would vote for the party, not the individual; and it would then be up to the party to select the best men and women for the job (Garret, November 1992). What a great idea! Sadly, those I spoke with believed this will never happen because Australian men are just too macho. It is a pity that a great country like Australia has such a reputation.

I wondered why most citizens just give up when they hear such ideas for social change. They complain, but they don't support or get out there and work for new ideas. How many of us sit at home and watch TV, and say, "Somebody ought to do something about that problem." One citizen can do a lot. For example, I was invited to a peace conference in Washington, D.C. Four hundred Russians attended. Ted Turner, who was the featured speaker, said that the Cold War was costing us ten trillion dollars! I was outraged by this figure. I said to myself, "Well what are you going to do about it then, Sondra Ray?" I volunteered myself to take rebirthing to Russia. I asked Rama Vernon, who had gone to the U.S.S.R. as a citizen diplomat, if I could go with her and support her. Suddenly I was committed. I was frightened because the old government was still in place, but I went anyway. It was the challenge of my career. And now I am pleased to give this report: The rebirthers I trained in Russia began to rebirth doctors who, in turn, did extensive research on themselves during rebirthing sessions. They proved scientifically that rebirthing rejuvenates the brain and the body! Rebirthing, in Russia, is on the rise.

In *New Teachings for an Awakening Humanity*, we are asked to wake up from our spiritual amnesia. The book reminds us that we are all collectively responsible as caretakers of the planet. The violence we express to other countries will return to us in suffering because of the law of karma. We can make *peace*, not war, profitable.

Political action can help establish a real brotherhood for humanity. It is only through Divine Love that we will finally know how to establish peace. Through Divine Love, we will tune into the Divine Plan for a new humanity. We need Divine Politics.

CLOSING

MAKING A DIFFERENCE WITH THIS INFORMATION

•

I PRAY THAT THIS MATERIAL INSPIRES YOU TO REACH FOR the highest in yourself, in your relationships, and in your work. I also ask you this: If you have, in fact, obtained value from this information, how can you give back to society for what you have learned? What are you willing to do in return?

Think about this spiritual principle: Nothing real can be increased except by sharing. We have an obligation to return to others what we have learned. For example, give spiritual books like this one to someone as a gift. Network! Network! Network!

Someone once said that, "Popular culture never gets above the power chakra." If this is so, it means that mass culture will never get beyond wanting power over others, movies will never stop their obsession with violence and power, and we are therefore doomed. I do not want to agree with that. I want to see the highest and the best in people.

If you have been in the New Age for awhile, what are doing to serve those who are not exposed to the liberating techniques you already know about? Get out there and make people conscious of their divinity. This is your task.

If you are "new" to the New Age, I totally acknowledge you for your courage in venturing into new territories. Please do not hide what you have learned because you are afraid of what people will think. Others in your community are just waiting for someone like you. Take the risk. Share.

So what are you going to do? How can you make a difference with what you have learned? How are you going to support the Divine Plan of the Divine Mother? Spiritual freedom means getting your soul out of bondage. There is no greater gift then this for you. Helping others to achieve spiritual freedom is the most important task we have. Each of us has to win this freedom for ourselves ultimately, but you can at least guide others to the right people, books, and seminars to facilitate the process.

Every day, begin by emanating the consciousness of the great ones such as Christ, Buddha, or Babaji. Then expand your consciousness to include your neighbors' interests, their well-being, and the well-being of everyone you will meet that day. Get in touch with your deep desire to help others, and ask the Holy Spirit what miracles he would like you to perform today. Opportunities are everywhere. Be alert. Robert Bly calls it the path of attention. He also reminds us to notice who we hate in the world. That hate is part of our shadow and can serve as a signal to do some self-analysis!

Open your heart. Start talking to people. Reach out. Give your love to all. *A Course in Miracles* says that you are among the ministers of God. Get busy. Become a spiritual warrior. Please contact us. Send me your ideas for a New Paradigm. Read on for addresses and events.

HOW TO HAVE A LOVING AND LASTING IDEAL RELATIONSHIP

by Lorrin L. Lee, PhD

1. **TALK.** Always in pleasant tones. No shouting or swearing at each other. Speak only positive words with gentleness and kindness. Communicate daily. This is the highest and most caring form of love.

2. **WALK TOGETHER** more. Take 30 minutes a day. To exercise, communicate, release emotions, share ideas, goals, and to clear up any misunderstandings. It's okay to hold hands, too!

3. **DO NEW AND DIFFERENT ACTIVITIES** together. Enjoy a new restaurant, a different dish, a concert, a unique vacation, attend a class together...something exciting both of you can plan and look forward to. Learn together and—you'll be happier.

4. **GIVE EACH OTHER GIFTS** often. Like a magazine subscription, a special book, a warm bath and massage, flowers, surprise experiences, favorite foods, and the many other special things your mate would enjoy and get excited about.

5. **WRITE LOVE NOTES.** Hide them around the home—in clothing, pockets, in the kitchen drawer and secret places. Send some to his or her working place. Write a passionate love letter. Express your love in writing on exquisite stationery. Attach a gift certificate or a crispy $100 bill. Use your imagination and make it a fun surprise. And do it often!

6. **DO NOT CRITICIZE, CONDEMN, OR COMPLAIN.** This is a NO-NO. Only praise and acknowledge the goodness in each other. There is no place for negativity in a loving and lasting relationship ever! Your mate will do the right thing as you lead by example.

7. **ACHIEVE AND MAINTAIN YOUR IDEAL FIGURE.** It is a gift to yourself and your mate. A healthy and attractive body also promotes a healthy relationship.

8. **ALLOW YOUR PARTNER TO BE RESPONSIBLE** for his or her life. He or she has the right to determine his or her own reality and destiny. Always respect that choice. Both of you can live your lives in your own way—harmoniously. Treasure each other's differences. Do your very best to make life easier and more fun for your mate.

9. **GROW TOGETHER** At the same speed and direction...by sharing similar ideas and activites. This will bond you together even more while building on fond memories. (People who don't grow together will complete their relationship and move on to lead separate lives. This is why most divorce.)

10. **DO NOT BE POSSESSIVE.** Don't act as though you "own" your mate. Support, encourage each other's way of living and individual interests. Be grateful in harmony.

11. **TREASURE YOU TIME TOGETHER.** It could be your last. Look at it this way and you'll always appreciate each other even more. Have NO reason for regrets. Spend time with each other doing all the things you both love to do. Do it now! Tomorrow may not come. So together—plan now for the best in the rest of your lives.

12. **IT IS OKAY TO DO WHAT PLEASES BOTH OF YOU.** In private, there are no limits what you can do together with each other, as long as both benefit and agree.

Whatever other people think of what you do or say is none of your business! So, go ahead experiment and satisfy each other to the limit!

13. **BE OPEN.** To new ideas, experiences, and relationships. This is the way for fun, growth, and expansion in your lives. The more you LEARN together, the better.

14. **FORGIVE AND LOVE.** Release the past at every moment. Live in the present. Plan for the future—together, and joyously!

15. **BE FREE** of resentments, anger, jealousy, hatred, and envy toward each other. This will open you up to even greater respect for each other. Be thankful for your mate's kindness.

16. **ELIMINATE ARGUING TOTALLY.** Anywhere, anytime. Especially while eating or in bed. Each person has a right to his or her own opinion. Respect each others ideas, philosophy, and outlook on life. Be a great listener!

17. **SMILE AND LAUGH** with each other. A prescription for aliveness and health. Don't take yourself or your mate too seriously. Lighten up and laugh more often. Remember, your smiles are true gifts to each other.

18. **LOOK INTO EACH OTHER'S EYES** often. See the love, truth, and beauty in your mate. The more you look into each other's eyes lovingly, the more you will love each other more deeply! Do this daily. It's very powerful and fun!

19. **TOUCH EACH OTHER TENDERLY**—every day. Hug. Kiss. Caress. These are wonderful ways to show caring and love. We ALL need it. More than we care to admit!

20. **DEVELOP A HEALTHY LIFESTYLE.** Good food promotes a healthier state of mind for a more meaningful relationship. Eat lots of fruits, vegetables, whole wheat, grains, hi-fiber, low-fat, low-calorie foods. Drink more

water. Get more rest. Keep yourself cleansed, nourished, and balanced.

21. **KEEP THINGS SIMPLE, NEAT, CLEAN AND ORGANIZED** —your home, car, kitchen, closets, rooms. This will help promote a setting for greater peace and happiness in your lives. It really works! Begin this— today!

22. **DRESS YOUR BEST.** Be appropriate, neat, clean, and proud of your appearance. How you look, especially in public, enhances your mate's choice and appearance too!

23. **SHARE IN FINANCIAL MATTERS.** If you are married, communicate with each other on all your finances. If you have a family business, be sure both are informed on profits, losses, expenses, etc. Set your financial priorities together. This will help to strengthen your relationship which is built on trust and sharing. Enjoy building your financial future together. This is important.

24. **ACCEPT EACH OTHER TOTALLY.** Exactly the way both of you are. Do not try to change each other's uniqueness. Allow your mate to change if and when he or she desires. This promotes everlasting peace.

25. **SAY: "I LOVE YOU."** Daily, many times. Especially when you wake up and before you go to sleep. Say it for the rest of your lives together. Never ever take love for granted. Express it verbally as well as with action. We all need to hear that magical phrase. It reaffirms how we feel at that moment. So, fill your lives with millions of moments of love—by saying: "I love you."

SONDRA RAY
INTERNATIONAL SEMINARS

Sondra Ray International offers the following seminars:

1. The New Relationships Training

This is the revised LRT (Loving Relationships Training). It covers: Sabotaging patterns and what to do about them; how your birth trauma affects your relationships; jealousy, sex, and other common problems; and how to apply spiritual enlightenment to your relationship. It also introduces the subject of Physical Immortality.

2. Relationships Reborn

This is Sondra's new training, presenting a New Paradigm for sacred relationships. Turn your relationship into a holy environment for the evolution of the soul. Let your relationship be a part of a spiritual path and rebirth yourselves into a new life together!

3. The Cooperation Training

Clear up sibling rivalry and competition so that you may have healthier and more productive relationships in business and in the work place. Release jealousy and destructive competitive patterns and enjoy the excitement of synergy. This training is great for companies.

4. The Liberation Training

An advanced wet-rebirthing training done, ideally, in an outdoor setting, preferably at a thermal hot springs.

Working with Divine Mother Energy, prayers are designed for each participant which are breathed into the body during wet-rebirthing sessions. This is ideal as a five-day training.

5. The Rejuvenation Training (Unlimited Life)

An intensive training on longevity and physical immortality. This very powerful training is offered on the island of Maui, Hawaii, every year. It can be given anywhere, however. Give up the unconscious death urge and stop the aging process.

6. Drinking the Divine Training

About *A Course in Miracles*, the most important book today, and how to apply its teachings to your life.

7. The Best of Sondra Ray

This training has four sections: (1) Relationships Technology, (2) Rebirthing, (3) Rejuvenation, and (4) the Metaphysics of Money.

8. The Divine Mother Conference

An international event usually held in Santa Fe, New Mexico (along with the Baca Ashram in Colorado). Uses the most powerful spiritual practices and methods of spiritual purification for working directly with the Divine Mother Energy.

9. The India Quest

Join Sondra in her annual visit to Babaji Ashrams in India: The lower ashram along the Ganges River and the upper ashram in the Himalayas. This awesome, one-month-long training includes a basic relationships training as part of the orientation and even a trip to the Taj Mahal. Please contact Peter and Dana Delong by phone or fax: (310) 798-2443.

10. Rebirth Trainings

Sondra had the privilege of being one of the first people in the world to be rebirthed and was one of the very first Rebirthers. She now trains rebirthers all over the world.

11. Leadership Trainings

Sondra is recruiting new trainers for her Relationships Trainings as she cannot possibly handle the current requests from countries all over the world. She would like to train leaders to, in turn, lead trainings in their own countries. If you are interested, please contact her at the addresses below.

Sondra is also available to speak for day-long or evening events on all of these subjects.

For more information on any of the above seminars, contact Sondra Ray c/o Sharda at (800) 690-5739, fax, (214) 690-7936, or write to: Box 835974, Richardson, Texas 75083-5974. In Europe, you may contact her through Diana Roberts, 9D Claverton St., London, England SW1V3AY, Telephone and fax: 44-1-71-834-6641.

Sondra's books:

> *I Deserve Love*
> *Rebirthing in the New Age*
> *Loving Relationships I*
> *The Only Diet There Is*
> *Ideal Birth*

Celebration of Breath

Birth and Relationships

Pure Joy

Drinking the Divine

Inner Communion

Interludes with the Gods

How to Be Chic, Fabulous, and Live Forever

Loving Relationships II

Essays on Creating Sacred Relationships

and coming soon...

Permanent Healing

Babaji Centers and Ashrams

AUSTRALIA
   c/o Jane Woods
   7 Village Low Road
   Benowa Waters, Queensland
   Australia 4217
   (Phone: 61-75-970-582)

INDIA
   Sri Trilok Singh (Muniraj)
   c/o Hind Traders
   Patel Chowk
   Hadlwani Dist Nanital

UNITED STATES
   Baca Haidakhandi Universal Ashram
   P.O. Box 9
   Crestone, Colorado 81131 USA
   (Phone: 719-256-4108)

ITALY
Centro Bhole Baba
Lisetti Carmi
Casella Postale 56
Cisternino Brindisi 72014

HOLLAND
Babaji Center
Valentynkade 45
1095 JJ Amsterdam NL

FRANCE
c/o Turkantam
La Touche Noire
36240 Gehee
France 54408437

SWITZERLAND
Centre of Unity
Schweibenalp
CH-3855 Brienz
(Phone: 036-512001)

BIBLIOGRAPHY

Anderson, Sherry R. and Patricia Hopkins. *Feminine Face of God.* New York: Bantam, 1992.

Baba, Meher. *Discourses* ed. by Eruch Jessawala et al. Myrtle Beach: Sheriar Foundation, 1987, 1995.

Chopra, Deepak. *Quantum Healing.* New York: Bantam, 1989.

Daly, Mary. *Beyond God the Father.* Boston: Beacon Press, 1985.

De Angelis, Barbara. *Secrets about Men Every Woman Should Know.* New York: Dell, 1991.

Faludi, Susan. *Backlash: The Undeclared War Against American Women.* New York: Doubleday, 1992.

Ferrini, Paul. *Love without Conditions—Reflections of the Christmind.* Santa Fe: Heartways Press, 1994.

Fortune, Dion. *Esoteric Philosophy of Love and Marriage.* London: Thorsen, 1987.

Foundation for Inner Peace. *A Course in Miracles.* Glenn Ellen: Foundation for Inner Peace, 1992.

Gray, John. *Men are from Mars, Women are from Venus.* New York: HarperCollins, 1994.

Isherwood, Christopher. *Vedanta for the Western World.* London: Unwin Books, 1963.

Kohn, Alfie. *No Contest: The Case Against Competition*. New York: Houghton Mifflin, 1986.

Mandel, Bob and Sondra Ray. *Birth and Relationships*. Berkeley: Celestial Arts Publishing, 1987.

Mandel, Bob. *Wake Up to Wealth*. Berkeley: Celestial Arts, 1994.

Paramahansa, Yogananda. *Man's Eternal Quest*. Los Angeles: Self Realization Fellowship, 1982.

Paramahansa, Yogananda. *Whispers of Eternity*. Los Angeles: Self Realization Fellowship, 1977.

Pittman, Frank S. *Man Enough, Fathers, Sons and Search for Masculinity*. New York: Putnam Publishing Group, 1994.

Price, John. *Abundance Book*. Boerne, TX: Quartus Books, 1987.

Ray, Sondra. *How to be Chic, Fabulous and Live Forever*. Berkeley: Celestial Arts, 1989.

Ray, Sondra. *Ideal Birth*. Berkeley: Celestial Arts, 1985.

Ray, Sondra. *Loving Relationships*. Berkeley: Celestial Arts, 1980.

Ray, Sondra. *Loving Relationships II*. Berkeley: Celestial Arts, 1992.

Ray, Sondra. *Pure Joy*. Berkeley: Celestial Arts, 1988.

Roskind, Robert. *In the Spirit of Business*. Berkeley: Celestial Arts, 1993.

Singh, Tara. *How to Raise a Child of God*. Los Angeles: Life Action Press, 1987.

Sutphen, Dick. *We Were Born Again to Be Together*. Ashland: Valley of the Sun Publishing, 1976.

Vaughan, Frances and Roger Walsh, *Accept This Gift*. Los Angeles: Jeremy Tarcher Inc., 1992.

Woolger, Roger. *Other Lives, Other Selves*. New York: Bantam, 1988.

Zitko, Howard. *New Age Tantra Yoga*. Arizona: World University, 1985.

Zukav, Gary. *Seat of the Soul*. New York: Simon and Schuster, 1990.

Magazines and Pamphlets

"Excuse me, I'm Networking." *Elle Magazine*, Australia edition, January 1994, pp. 66-68.

Garratt, Isabell. *Ita Magazine*, "What Did You Say." November, 1992.

Hazelton Clinic Pamphlet._____

Kagy, Tom. "Asian Success Secrets." *Transpacific Magazine*, pp. 28-33, 81 and 82.

Osho, "From Sex to Super Consciousness." *Golden Age Magazine*, Issue 11, pp. 16-18.

"Running Scared." *Elle Magazine*, Australia edition, March, 1994, pages 79-92.

"Your Guide to Equality." *New Woman Magazine*, Australia edition, March 1994, pp. 44-58.

Worley, Father Lloyd. "Esoteric Side of Love and Marriage," Geneva, Nebraska: St. George Press.